RICHARD PRESCOTT

Officially Dead

Founding Editor: John Milne

The Macmillan Readers provide a choice of enjoyable reading materials for learners of English. The series is published at six levels – Starter, Beginner, Elementary, Pre-intermediate, Intermediate and Upper.

Level control
Information, structure and vocabulary are controlled to suit the students' ability at each level.

The number of words at each level:

Starter	about 300 basic words
Beginner	about 600 basic words
Elementary	about 1100 basic words
Pre-intermediate	about 1400 basic words
Intermediate	about 1600 basic words
Upper	about 2200 basic words

Vocabulary
Some difficult words and phrases in this book are important for understanding the story. Some of these words are explained in the story and some are shown in the pictures. From Pre-intermediate level upwards, words are marked with a number like this: …³. These words are explained in the Glossary at the end of the book.

Contents

The People in This Story

Colin Fenton

Julie Fenton

John Bentley

Linda Bentley

Frankie Simpson

Mr Booker

Mark Ashwood

Rob

Jenny

Maggie

Mr Rose

1

The Meeting

Colin Fenton was lying on the bed in his hotel room, wishing that he was somewhere else. The window was open and he could hear the constant sound of traffic outside.

The hotel was in Brentwood, a small town in Essex, just beyond the eastern suburbs[4] of London. Colin was in Brentwood to teach a computer software[1] course to the administrative staff of a company called Sutton Chemicals. This kind of teaching was always dull, tedious work, and today – the first day of the course – it had been particularly dull and tedious. By the afternoon, Colin had been exhausted. Now it was good to lie on the bed in the semi-darkness.

The evening air was cool and damp. Slowly, Colin got up off the bed and went to close the window. He stared out over the hotel car-park towards the wide, busy street beyond, while he wondered where he could go to eat dinner.

He had a shower and put on some casual clothes. He phoned his home in Bath, about 200 kilometres away to the west, but his wife wasn't in the house. Then Colin remembered that she had been going to travel to see some clients that afternoon. She'd probably had to work late – she often did.

'I'll phone her after dinner,' he thought.

Colin and his wife, Julie, were partners in business. Their company, C.J.F. Software Solutions, developed computer programs and sold them to a number of large businesses. Colin looked after the company's finances, the marketing of the computer software, and the organization of training courses. Julie, was a software developer.

Colin left his hotel room and went to find somewhere to

5

eat. The hotel didn't have a restaurant, but earlier in the day Colin had seen a pub which had a restaurant attached, just down the street. He decided to walk there.

The food and wine were excellent. At last, Colin began to relax. So after the meal, instead of going straight back to the hotel to have an early night, he went into the bar of the pub. It was noisy and crowded, but Colin didn't care about that. In one corner of the bar there was a large television set. A football match was showing, and most of the customers were watching it. Colin bought a drink and tried to find an empty seat. As he was looking round the crowded room, he saw something that almost made him drop his glass. He walked towards a man who was standing at the other end of the bar.

'For a moment, I thought I was looking in a mirror,' he said.

The other man was shocked too. The two of them stood facing each other. It was strange – unreal. Then they both laughed.

The two men were unbelievably alike. They were both in their late thirties, they had almost identical features, they even had the same hairstyle. Colin was perhaps slightly heavier, but otherwise the two men were doubles.

'We could be twin brothers,' the other man said.

They introduced themselves. The other man's name was John Bentley. He had a soft London accent[4].

'There's a seat free at our table, if you'd like to join us,' he said. 'I must introduce you to my wife.'

Linda Bentley was sitting on a long seat in the corner farthest from the television. She moved along the seat to make room for Colin.

'It's incredible,' she said, looking at Colin and her husband. 'You two are identical – you're perfect doubles!'

Linda was dressed in black clothes. She had fair hair, large green eyes, and a broad smile. She wore a lot of make-up and

'You two are identical – you're perfect doubles!'

she wore a lot of heavy gold jewellery. Her skirt, Colin noticed, was very short indeed. She could not have looked less like his own wife, but he liked the way she looked.

'I've not seen you in here before, Colin,' John Bentley said. 'Where are you from?'

'Bath,' Colin said. 'My wife and I own a small computer software company there. I'm in Brentwood for a couple of days, teaching a course.'

'Oh, I don't know anything about computer software,' Linda said. 'You must be very clever.'

She smiled at him and Colin laughed. 'No,' he said, 'my wife's the clever one.'

Colin enjoyed being with the Bentleys. He liked their friendly way of talking. Over the next hour, he drank more than he had planned to drink. As a result, he became very talkative. But after some time, he noticed that John Bentley had become silent. Bentley was probably bored with hearing him talk, Colin thought. But Linda kept asking him questions about his business.

When it was time to leave the pub, Colin shook hands with the Bentleys and they wished one another goodnight.

'Will you be here in Brentwood again?' Linda asked Colin, as they walked out into the cool night air.

'Yes, I will, actually,' Colin said. 'I've got another two-day course to teach at Sutton Chemicals in about a month's time.'

'Oh, so perhaps we'll be seeing each other again then!' she said. 'That would be great.' Her eyes opened wide with pleasure.

'Yes,' Colin said. 'We must meet. I'd love to see you again – both of you.'

Colin turned into the street, and John and Linda Bentley walked towards a white van at the far side of the pub car-park.

'Goodnight, Colin!' Linda called.

As soon as Colin Fenton was out of sight, the Bentleys

started arguing. John, who had drunk rather a lot of beer that evening, began to shout at his wife.

'What did you think you were doing?' he yelled. 'What's your game[3]? Why were you flirting[4] with that guy?'

When he was angry, John Bentley sometimes became violent and hit his wife. But now, some people were crossing the car-park behind them, talking in loud voices and laughing. Linda knew her husband wouldn't hit her while there were people near.

'Shut up,' she said. 'Give me the keys to the van.'

John ignored her and began opening the driver's door. She grabbed the keys from him and pushed him out of the way. She got into the driver's seat and waited for him to walk round to the passenger's side. He got slowly into the van.

They were silent as she drove away from the pub. But after a minute, Linda touched her husband's hand.

'Don't be an idiot, John,' she said.

John Bentley didn't reply. He just stared out of the window. They were driving along a wide road lined with[4] shops. It had started to rain and the street lamps were reflected on the wet road and pavements.

Linda turned into a side street. 'That guy will be useful to us, you'll see,' she said. 'That's why we must make sure that we see him again.'

John turned to look at her. 'What do you mean?' he said.

'You and he are identical, John,' she said. 'That's interesting, don't you think?'

Her husband didn't understand her.

A minute later, Linda slowed down and turned onto the drive in front of the garage of their small house. The van's headlights shone onto the garage door.

'You can forget about small-time thieving[2] now, John,' Linda said. 'If you do one big, easy robbery now, we'll be rich for the rest of our lives!'

'I'm going straight now, Linda,' John said. 'I'm finished with thieving – you know that. I don't want to go to prison again.'

'You won't go to prison this time,' his wife replied quickly. 'There's no way you'll get caught.'

———

When Colin Fenton got back to his hotel room, it was too late to phone his wife.

'Oh, well,' he thought. 'I'll be back home in Bath tomorrow night anyway. It doesn't matter now.'

The idea of another day teaching the administrative staff of Sutton Chemicals was thoroughly tedious. He didn't want to think about it. He thought instead about Linda Bentley. The only good thing about coming back to Sutton Chemicals for another course was that he might get a chance to see her again.

2

The Business

It was a cold, wet Monday morning in late October, two weeks after Colin had taught the training course at Sutton Chemicals. The trees that lined the streets of Bath were bare. Dead leaves lay on the pavements. Colin shivered as he got into his car. He picked a cassette from a pile on the passenger's seat, put it into the player, and started the car engine. A moment later, an old blues song was coming from the stereo.

Colin and Julie always went to work in separate cars. They left home at different times in the mornings and arrived home at different times in the evenings. During the day, they hardly saw each other. They were busy with their own jobs. Both of them regularly travelled to see clients – Julie to sort out[3] their technical problems, Colin to sell the software and teach training courses. But they rarely travelled together.

Today was one of the rare days when they were both going to be in Bath all day. But before he went to the office, Colin had an appointment that he wasn't looking forward to.

He drove to the eastern side of the city, parked his BMW, and hurried through the rain to a low office block. Outside one of the ground floor offices was a brass sign with the words, *D.S.T. Booker – Accountant.*

Colin opened the door and walked in. A girl was working at a desk with six filing trays, a computer and two telephones on it. 'Mr Booker's expecting me,' Colin told her.

'Yes, that's fine,' the girl replied. 'Please go through.'

Colin went through a door into another room. Mr Booker was bent over his desk, reading some papers. He wore very thick glasses and he held the papers close to his pale face. He

11

looked like a man in pain.

Colin sat down and pushed a folder of financial documents across the desk. Booker slowly raised his head, opened the folder and glanced briefly through the documents.

'You're going to lose money for the second year running[4], Mr Fenton,' he said. 'You've got to do something about this quickly or you'll go out of business[1].'

'I know the situation isn't good at the moment,' Colin replied. 'We're short of cash. But the situation's only temporary.'

'Well,' Booker said, 'the facts are clear enough. This year, you've earned around £40,000 so far. But last year, you spent more than £150,000. And you'll spend more or less the same this year. Your business won't survive unless there are some large orders coming in soon.'

Colin was silent. He looked down at the floor.

Booker leant forward. 'And you haven't got any large orders coming in, have you?' he said. He seemed almost pleased.

'We're developing some important new software for Jackman's, the big insurance brokers[1],' Colin said. 'It's for use at their head office, in Manchester. It's a valuable contract.'

'Have you signed the contract already?' Booker asked.

'Well, no, actually,' Colin said. 'The people at Jackman's are waiting for the results of some tests. We still have to sort out a few technical problems with the software. But in a few months, everything will be ready.'

Booker smiled. 'I see,' he said. 'Well, you'll need to earn about £20,000 between now and the end of the year, if you want your company to survive.'

'I've arranged a loan[1] at the bank,' Colin said.

Booker began collecting his papers. He stood up slowly. The accountant's body was stiff and his shoulders were bent.

He took the papers from his desk and put them into a brown

'You've got to do something about this quickly or you'll go out of business.'

folder. Colin noticed that Booker's hands were trembling slightly as he put the folder into a filing cabinet.

'Bank loans are trouble,' Booker said, pushing the heavy drawer shut. 'And you need real orders now, not possible orders in a few months' time. You need cash now, or you'll go out of business.'

———

When Colin arrived at his own office, his wife was getting ready to leave. Julie had an appointment with a client on the other side of the city. Her desk was covered with papers, computer books and floppy disks[1]. She was sorting through them, putting what she needed into her briefcase.

Julie saw Colin looking at her. 'Is everything OK?' she asked. 'You've been to see Booker this morning, haven't you? What did he say?'

'Oh, nothing much,' Colin said. 'He just wanted me to take him some documents he needed.'

'Fine,' Julie said. 'Well, I'd better be going[3]. I don't expect I'll be back here today. I'll see you at home tonight.'

Colin took off his jacket and sat at his desk. He looked through the glass partition between his and Julie's room and the main part of the office. Rob and Jenny, the two programmers[1], were busy at their computers. Near the door of the main office, Maggie was sitting at her desk. Maggie was the secretary, telephonist and general office helper. She had been with Colin and Julie ever since they had started C.J.F. Software Solutions, five years before.

Colin opened the letters that Maggie had put on his desk earlier in the morning. Among them was a letter from his bank manager. The letter explained the details of the bank loan that Colin had arranged the previous week.

At the bottom of the pile of long business envelopes there was a smaller envelope. Colin's name and the address of the company were hand-written neatly on it. Colin opened the

14

envelope. The paper he pulled out smelt of perfume.

Dear Colin,

You'll probably be surprised to get a letter from me. I found your company's address in the Yellow Pages[4]. I just wanted to remind you that we'd love to see you when you next come to Brentwood. I think you said you would be here again in a few weeks' time. Perhaps this time you could have dinner with us at our house?

We really enjoyed that evening we spent together. Your funny stories made us laugh so much. Please phone me on 0033 23456 before your next visit, so that we can arrange to meet.

> *Hoping to see you again soon.*
> *Best wishes,*

> > *Linda Bentley*

Colin held the letter close to his face. The perfume was the one which Linda Bentley had been wearing that Wednesday night in the pub in Brentwood.

Colin didn't know what to think about the letter. What did Linda mean by 'your funny stories'? He had talked a lot that evening, but he couldn't remember telling any funny stories. Well, not many, anyway!

The letter could be embarrassing for him, Colin thought. He didn't want Julie to see it. He quickly read through the letter again and he noticed that the number was for a mobile phone. He tore off the part of the letter with the phone number on it, and put the piece of paper in his wallet[4]. He tore the rest of the letter into small pieces and put them into the waste-paper bin beside his desk.

3

The Plan

Linda Bentley was thirty-three years old and she was good-looking. She was used to getting what she wanted. She had made an important decision very early in her life – since there was no one to look after her, she would make sure that she looked after herself.

Linda had been born in Glasgow, the largest city in Scotland. She had no brothers or sisters and she didn't know who her father was. Until she was twelve, Linda had lived with her mother in a damp, dark flat. The flat had a bedroom – which was the living-room too – a small kitchen, and a bathroom. Linda's mother usually went out in the evenings, leaving her alone. Sometimes her mother brought men home with her, and then she told Linda to sleep on the floor in the kitchen.

When she was twelve, Linda's mother disappeared and, after that, Linda never saw her again. She didn't know where her mother had gone, or what had happened to her, and she didn't care. An aunt and uncle took Linda into their home and they tried to love her and care for her. But the girl no longer understood what love was. As soon as she was eighteen years old, she left Glasgow and went south to London.

She found a job in a pub called the Red Lion in Ilford, in east London. That was where she met John Bentley. John was a likeable young man and a good-looking one. He was an orphan, so he and Linda had something in common[4]. But Linda had learnt to look after herself and John had not. So Linda tried to look after him. He was working as a lorry driver at that time, and he always seemed to have plenty of money. He spent a lot

16

of it on presents for Linda. She enjoyed getting the presents and she didn't ask where the money came from. A year after their first meeting, John and Linda got married.

When – a few months later – John was sent to prison, Linda found out where his money had been coming from. Now she was alone in London, but there was no point in going back to Glasgow. Her aunt and uncle had moved to Spain. So Linda decided to stay in London and wait for John. But she needed a change, so she started looking for a new job. She soon found one in a large jewellery shop in a fashionable part of London. The shop was called Sandwell's. Linda's job there was much better paid than the work in the pub, and it was much more pleasant too.

When John Bentley came out of prison, he was determined to stay away from his old friends. He decided to go straight. He had hated being locked in a cell for most of each day, and he didn't want to go back to prison. Linda persuaded Mr Rose, the manager at Sandwell's, to give her husband a job. The manager knew about John's time in prison, but he gave the young man a chance to live an honest life[2]. Later that year, John and Linda moved into the small rented[4] house near Brentwood where they still lived.

———

Early one evening, a few weeks after she had sent the letter to Colin, Linda Bentley was in her kitchen, preparing a meal. As she put some fish into a large pan, her mobile phone began to ring. She quickly wiped her hands and put the phone to her ear. John was in the living-room, watching television. He couldn't hear Linda's conversation.

'So you'll be in Brentwood next week,' Linda said. 'That's great, Colin! How long will you be staying?'

'Two nights,' Colin said. 'We could meet on Wednesday or Thursday evening.'

Linda thought for a moment. 'Wednesday will be best for me,' she said. 'Can we can meet in the same pub, at around six-thirty? Then later, you can come here for a meal with us.'

'Yes, that's fine! I'll see you next Wednesday, then,' Colin said.

Linda switched her phone off and put it in her handbag. She smiled to herself. Wednesday was certainly the best day for what she had in mind. John would be away from home that night!

Soon the fish was ready. Linda switched off the cooker and turned round with the pan in her hand. John was standing in the kitchen doorway.

'I heard your phone ring,' he said. 'Who were you talking to?'

'No one,' Linda replied. 'Somebody called a wrong number.'

She lifted the pieces of fish onto two plates and added some vegetables. 'Sit down and eat this while it's hot,' she said.

———

On the evening of the following Tuesday, Colin Fenton left his home in Bath and travelled to Brentwood. He booked into the same hotel, ready to start work early in the morning.

The next evening, after a day spent with the administrative staff at Sutton Chemicals, he was beginning to regret his agreement to meet the Bentleys. He was tired, and he decided to phone them to say he couldn't meet them after all. But when he looked at his watch he saw that it was too late. It was almost six o'clock already, and he had agreed to meet his friends at the pub at six-thirty. He would have to go to the pub, eat his meal at their home as quickly as he could, and leave early.

This time, the pub wasn't crowded. There was no football on the television and the bar was nearly empty. A few people were sitting at tables, drinking and talking.

Linda Bentley was waiting for him, sitting on her own at a

table in a corner. She had a glass of orange juice in front of her. Colin walked across the room towards her. She stood up and shook his hand.

'Hello,' she said. 'I'm glad you could come.'

She was wearing a black dress, made of shiny material. It was tight-fitting and very short.

'It's good to see you, Linda,' Colin said. 'Can I get you another drink?'

'No, it's OK, thanks. I haven't finished this yet,' she replied, touching her glass.

'What about John?' Colin said, looking round the room. 'Where is he?'

'I'm afraid it's just you and me tonight,' Linda said. 'John can't come. He's driven his van to Liverpool with some mates[3].'

'Liverpool?' Colin said, surprised.

'Yes. They've gone to a football match,' Linda replied. 'John's football mad. He supports West Ham United. He goes to watch all their matches. West Ham are playing Liverpool Football Club tonight.'

'You should have sent me a message,' Colin said. 'We could have met another time.'

Linda smiled at him. 'I wanted to see you tonight, John. Go and get yourself a drink,' she said.

After a few drinks, they left the pub and Linda drove them back to her house in her red Ford Escort. Everything was ready for dinner. There was a small vase of flowers in the middle of the table and a glass bowl full of water on which candles floated.

While Linda finished preparing the food, Colin looked at the framed photographs on the sideboard[4] in the living-room. They were mostly pictures of John and Linda on holiday in various places. But one photograph showed an elderly couple sitting in a sunny Mediterranean garden. Colin picked it up and looked at it.

Linda came into the room, carrying a tray of pasta and salad. Colin pointed to the photo. 'Your parents?' he asked.

'No, my aunt and uncle,' Linda replied. 'But they were like parents to me. They looked after me when I was a teenager in Glasgow. My uncle is dead now, but my aunt still lives in Spain. It's too cold and wet for her in Scotland.'

'Do you see your aunt often?' asked Colin.

'No, I haven't seen her for years. John doesn't like the heat in Spain,' Linda replied, laughing. 'But we might go to see her soon.'

They spent the next couple of hours eating, laughing, and getting to know each other[4]. Colin was soon feeling much better, and he was glad that he had come. Suddenly, he found himself looking straight into Linda's large green eyes. She smiled at him and looked down at the table, pretending to be embarrassed.

It was late when they finished their meal. Then they sat in armchairs, drinking coffee. After the second cup, Linda leant back in her chair and said calmly, 'Colin, do you want to earn £10,000 for one evening's easy work?'

This simple question took Colin completely by surprise. He'd been expecting a proposal[4], but a very different one. He laughed. 'I don't buy lottery tickets,' he said.

'I'm serious, Colin,' Linda said. 'And I'm not talking about buying lottery tickets.'

She got up and came to sit on the floor next to his chair. She smiled at him and touched his hand. 'I'm talking about £10,000 in cash. It's yours, if you want it.'

Colin sat up straight and removed Linda's hand from his own hand. 'What's going on?' he said nervously. 'What do you want from me?'

'Nothing, Colin,' she said quickly. 'I was joking.' She stood

'... £10,000 in cash. It's yours, if you want it.'

up. 'Let's have some more coffee.'

'You weren't joking,' Colin said. 'You'd better tell me what this is about.'

'You're right, I wasn't joking,' she replied. 'But I'm not sure that I should tell you. Perhaps I've made a mistake.'

Colin finished his coffee and stood up. 'OK. You'd better take me back to my hotel,' he said. 'It really is late. It's past midnight.'

Colin got up and went into the hall to get his coat. When he came back into the living-room, Linda Bentley's eyes were wet and tears were running down her cheeks. 'I'm sorry, Colin,' she said. She cried quietly. Colin put his arms around her and held her for a moment. Then he kissed the tears on her cheeks and stroked her hair. 'It's all right, Linda,' he said.

Linda stopped crying and pulled herself away from him. 'You must think I'm very stupid,' she said. 'I'll get my coat and take you back to your hotel. I'm so sorry I spoilt a lovely evening.'

She went into the hall and took her coat from a cupboard. Colin followed her. When she turned round, Colin was right behind her. He took the coat from her and dropped it on the floor. She looked at him, her eyes wide open. Colin held her arms, pulled her very close to him and kissed her on the mouth.

'You can take me back to the hotel early tomorrow morning,' he said. 'The evening's not spoilt at all.'

Early next morning, Colin and Linda had some coffee and toast together. Then Linda drove Colin back to his hotel. It was only seven-fifteen and the roads were clear. It was a cold, sunny morning. They talked about what each of them was going to do during the day. But they both knew they were avoiding talking about the previous night. Suddenly, they both became silent. Colin stared out of the window. They were driving past trees that were white with frost[4]. Colin turned and looked at Linda. At last, Linda smiled at him and spoke.

'What are you thinking about, Colin?' she asked.

'It was a strange evening, wasn't it?' he replied.

Linda nodded.

'You planned it all, didn't you?' Colin said.

'Do you mind if I did?' she asked.

Colin thought for a moment. 'No, I don't think I do,' he said. Then he added, 'And what about the £10,000? You *were* serious about that, weren't you?'

They had reached Colin's hotel. Linda drove onto the car-park and switched off the car engine. 'My husband is going to need an alibi[2],' she said. 'You can provide one for him. It's as simple as that.'

'What do you mean?'

'You and John are identical. All *you* have to do is pretend to be John for a night.'

'While John does a robbery, am I right?'

'Right.'

'What's he going to steal?'

'I can't tell you that.'

'Linda, I need to know,' Colin said. 'It won't be an *armed* robbery, will it? Nobody will carry a gun?'

'No one will get killed or hurt, Colin.'

'What's the plan?' Colin asked. 'Is John going to rob a bank?'

'No,' Linda said. 'And you don't need to know any more about it.'

'Yes, I do, Linda,' Colin insisted. 'I have to know what risk[4] I'll be taking. I don't want anybody to get hurt. And I don't want to spend years of my life in prison.'

Linda thought for a moment. 'All right, Colin,' she said, 'I'll tell you the plan. John and I work in a jewellery shop. We know all about the security systems[2] there. John will be able to get inside the shop at night without setting off the alarm. He'll smash a window and set off the alarm as he's leaving. We hope that the police will think it's an ordinary break-in[2]. But John has a criminal record[2], and the police might suspect him if he doesn't have an alibi. He'll need a really good alibi. You can provide him with it.'

'I understand,' Colin said. 'When do you plan to do this?'

'We haven't chosen a date yet. We can make our plans fit with yours,' Linda replied. 'You travel a lot because of your work, you told us that. One day, when you're somewhere a long way from London, you can stay in a hotel using John's name. That will give John a perfect alibi. And only the three of us will ever know how the robbery was done.'

'You've planned this all very carefully, haven't you?'

'When I want something, I make sure I get it,' Linda said.

Colin thought about the previous evening.

'Yes, you do,' he agreed in a cold voice. 'What about the money – the £10,000?'

'We can pay you a few thousand in advance,' Linda said. 'You'll get the rest soon after the robbery.'

'I might be able to help you. But I need some time to think about this,' said Colin.

'OK,' Linda said. 'You've got my phone number.'

'I'll be in touch[3],' said Colin.

He got out of the car and watched Linda drive away. Then he went up to his room to get the things he needed for his day at Sutton Chemicals.

4

The Journey

A few weeks later, Linda Bentley got the phone call she had been expecting. She was hurrying back to the jewellery shop after her lunch-break. It was nearly Christmas and the London streets were crowded with shoppers. Linda's mobile phone rang inside her bag. She opened her bag and lifted the phone to her ear. She heard Colin say, 'All right, I'll do it.'

'Good, I knew you would,' she replied. 'We'll need a few weeks to get everything ready.'

'That's fine,' Colin said. 'I'll be in Manchester in about four weeks' time. That'll be the second week in January. We can arrange John's alibi for then.'

'Phone me again next week, Colin,' Linda said. 'We'll fix the dates and times then.'

Linda put her phone back inside her handbag and smiled. She pushed her way through the crowds and she ran down some steps into an Underground station. Her only problem now was to tell John about the plan. Her husband still knew nothing about her second meeting with Colin Fenton.

———

That evening, the Bentleys were sitting in their kitchen, eating dinner. John had a newspaper on the table and he was reading the sports pages while he ate. Linda put her hand on his arm.

'John, do you remember our friend Colin?' she said.

'Who?' John said, not looking up.

'You know, the guy who looks just like you,' Linda said.

'What about him?' John turned the page of the newspaper and folded it.

'He's agreed to give you an alibi.'

Linda stood up and carried her plate to the sink, so that she did not have to look at John.

John put the newspaper down and pushed his chair back. 'When did you speak to him?' he said.

'A couple of weeks ago,' Linda said, filling the sink with water. 'I met him in the pub. He was teaching a course at that chemical company.'

'Was that when I was in Liverpool?'

Linda knew that John was angry and jealous. She didn't answer him.

'You waited for me to be out of the way!' John shouted. 'I expect you had a great time together, didn't you? Come on, answer me!'

Linda heard a plate smash against the tiled floor.

'What was it? Dinner in the pub? Or did you come back here for dinner? And what else did you come back here for?'

John was furious. He stood up suddenly and his chair fell back and hit the floor. Linda cried out in pain as John grabbed her arms and began shaking her.

'I don't *need* an alibi!' John shouted. 'No alibi! Forget it! I told you before. I'm not going to rob the shop. I'm going straight now.'

Linda was screaming with pain. She pushed her husband with all her strength. John crashed into the kitchen table and then fell hard against the wall, hitting his head against it with a loud crack. Linda turned, breathing fast. She stared at the blood-stain on the white wall. Below it, John was lying on the floor, holding his head.

'Don't you ever do that to me again!' Linda shouted.

She left him there and went upstairs to wash. Her arms ached and she could hardly move them. Where John had grabbed her, there were two large, dark bruises on her skin.

Linda went to the bedroom, got into bed and closed her eyes. After some time, she heard John moving about downstairs, cleaning up in the kitchen. Later she heard him come up the stairs, go to the bathroom and have a shower. When he got into the bed, he didn't speak to her. But he didn't go to sleep.

After half an hour, Linda said quietly, 'We mustn't waste any time, John. Tomorrow, you'd better go and see Frankie Simpson at the Red Lion. Talk to him about the jewellery. He'll fence[2] it for us. Don't tell him where you're getting it from. Just tell him you want him to sell more than a million pounds' worth of jewellery. Okay?'

John didn't answer.

'Okay?' Linda repeated.

'Okay,' John said at last.

———

Towards the end of December, Colin made the final arrangements with Linda. The date for the robbery was arranged for 10th January. Now that all the plans were made, Colin suddenly understood the risk he was taking. But he tried not to worry, telling himself that it was only an exciting game. After all, the money he was going to be paid would save his company.

Colin and Julie spent the Christmas holidays visiting Julie's brother and his family in Devon. No one noticed that Colin was a little quieter than usual.

One morning in early January, Colin and Julie were in the office together, talking about the big project at Jackman's, the insurance brokers. Julie was still testing the software, but that morning the Fentons were discussing a report that Julie had just given Colin. The report was full of charts showing the results of the latest tests.

'These figures look good, Julie,' Colin said. 'When I show the people at Jackman's these charts, I'm sure they'll be very impressed. I'm going to see Jim Slater in Manchester next week. It should be easy to convince him to purchase the software now.'

'I'd better come with you,' Julie said. 'There'll be technical details to discuss.'

'I can do that,' Colin said. 'Leave it with me.'

'No, Colin,' Julie said. 'I should be in Manchester with you. You know how fussy[4] Slater is about details. We've got to do this properly. Jackman's could become our biggest client.'

Colin stood up and looked out of the window. He was thinking quickly. He couldn't allow Julie to come to Manchester with him – not this time.

He turned round and said, 'I'll just have preliminary talks with Slater. We won't discuss the details this time. Of course you'll be with me when we have *that* discussion. I've already fixed this appointment, so I'll go alone this time. Anyway, I've got other people to visit up in the Manchester area. I'll be away for a couple of days.'

'You should have spoken to me first, Colin,' Julie said. 'You shouldn't have arranged an appointment before seeing my report on the latest tests.'

'Slater phoned *me*, Julie. The meeting was *his* idea,' Colin said. He was surprised at how easy it was for him to lie. 'Slater asked to see me, so I fixed it with him.'

––––––

On Tuesday 10th January, Colin worked at the office in Bath all day. Then at about five-thirty he went home to pack his suitcase for his trip to Manchester. He changed into casual clothes – jeans, sweater and an old sports jacket. He didn't want to look like a businessman when he arrived at his hotel later that evening. He wanted to look like John Bentley.

He was ready to leave his house by six o'clock. He put his mobile phone in one of the pockets of his jacket. As he stepped out of the house and walked towards his car, he felt an icy wind on his face. Fine powdery snow blew across the drive. Colin put his case in the boot[4] of his BMW, got into the car and started the engine.

Instead of driving towards the M5 – the quickest route to Manchester – Colin made his way to the M4, and turned east towards London. He stopped at a service area[4] near Swindon, to buy petrol and have a quick cup of tea. He was hungry but there was no time to eat.

The motorway was quite busy, and the snow was falling faster. It was nearly eight o'clock when Colin reached the last exit[4] before the M4 crosses the M25, the motorway that circles London. He left the M4, and a few minutes later, he drove into a lay-by[4] off a small road. He saw the Bentleys' red Ford Escort waiting there and he parked next to it. He got out into the snow and the freezing air, and approached the other car. Linda Bentley opened one of the rear doors for him to get in. He sat beside her.

'Exactly on time,' Linda said. Colin nodded. Then he said hello to John Bentley, who was sitting in the driver's seat. Linda handed Colin her husband's driving licence.

'What's this for?' Colin asked.

'You may need it,' Linda said. 'The alibi must be perfect. If you're stopped by the police, you must show them John's documents, not your own. We can't take any risks. What if there's an accident? We'll need *your* licence too, for the same reason.'

Colin took his driving licence from his pocket and gave it to Linda. 'What about my money?' he said.

Linda took out a thick envelope from her bag and handed it to Colin. 'That's £5000 in twenty-pound notes,' she said. 'Count it.'

Colin did.

'Right,' Linda said. 'Did you book a hotel room in Manchester as John Bentley?'

Again Colin nodded.

'Good. Phone us at about eleven-thirty, when you get to the hotel. Once we know that you've arrived, and that the alibi's OK, we can get moving. Is everything clear?'

'Yes,' Colin said.

'OK, get your case,' Linda said.

They all got out of the Bentleys' car. Colin opened the boot of his own car and took out his case. Colin and John exchanged car keys.

'We'll meet here, at the same time on Thursday,' Linda said. 'You'll get your car and driving licence back then and you'll get the rest of your money too.' She smiled briefly. 'We'll wait for your call at about eleven-thirty tonight, then.'

'Yes, fine,' Colin said.

Colin watched while John and Linda drove off in his BMW. He put the envelope of money safely in an inside pocket of his suitcase and zipped the pocket closed. He put the case in the boot of the Escort then he got into the driving seat. He started the engine and drove back towards the motorway. A few minutes later, he was driving along the M4 towards the junction[4] with the M25.

'We'll wait for your call at about eleven-thirty tonight.'

5

The Accident

The M25 was very busy and the traffic moved very slowly indeed. Colin didn't need to stay on that motorway for long, because he was driving to the junction with the M40. He hoped to make better progress when he turned onto the M40 and started to drive north-west towards Birmingham. But instead, the traffic on the M40 was even worse than on the M25. Roadworks[4], and the high winds and heavy snow, reduced the traffic speed to less than 50 kph. Time was passing and Colin began to wonder whether he could reach Manchester that night. He decided that the only thing to do was to leave the motorway at the next exit, and drive on smaller roads north towards Birmingham. Beyond Birmingham, he could join the M6, which he hoped would be less busy, and drive to Manchester on that.

As soon as he had left the M40, Colin was sure he had made the right decision. After a few minutes, he was racing along quiet country roads.

Then the accident happened. It was just after nine o'clock. The road in front of him was clear and Colin put his foot down on the accelerator. There were no street lights, and the night was very dark. High hedges and tall trees lined the road. Beyond the hedges, the fields seemed black. The narrow road curved sharply ahead. Colin turned his steering-wheel, but suddenly the car was out of control[4]. It spun round, rolled over, then crashed into a huge tree by the side of the road.

Another car had been following the red Escort for several miles – a blue Volvo. The car's driver witnessed[4] the accident. Mark Ashwood slowed down as he watched the car spin and roll over. When it hit the tree there was a dreadful noise of tearing metal and breaking glass.

Mark stopped his car behind the wrecked Escort. Leaving his engine running and turning his headlights full on, he jumped out of his car and hurried towards the wreck. The road, he noticed, was covered in ice.

The accident looked serious. The car lay on its roof. The Escort was a mass⁴ of torn metal. Broken glass lay on the icy road and on the snow-covered grass by the side of the road. The front of the car was against the trunk of the tree. There seemed no hope for the driver.

Mark looked inside the wrecked car. A man was trapped in the driver's seat, the steering-wheel pressing into his chest. He was still alive. Mark could hear him groaning quietly.

Mark pulled at the twisted metal that had been the driver's door, but it would not move. Cutting equipment⁴ would be needed to free the injured man. Mark tried to think what to do. He was a long way from a phone box, and he was not carrying a mobile. He didn't want to leave the injured man alone. But he could do nothing to free him without help.

After a minute, Mark heard a lorry approaching. He stood in the middle of the road, waving his arms. The lorry stopped and the driver looked out of the cab. He saw the wreckage and shook his head.

'Will you drive to a phone box please?' Mark shouted to him. 'This is an emergency!'

'There's no need, mate,' the lorry driver called back. 'I've got a mobile phone.'

'Then please phone for the emergency services⁴ quickly! There's a man trapped in there. We'll need a fire crew and an ambulance, as well as the police.'

While the lorry driver was phoning, Mark went back to the injured man. After a half a minute, the lorry driver called down

'… Please phone for the emergency services quickly! There's a man trapped in there.'

from his cab.

'An ambulance is on its way,' he said. 'Do you need my help here?'

'There's nothing you can do. I'll wait till help arrives.'

'Then I'll move on. I'm blocking the road with the lorry.'

As the lorry moved slowly away, Mark looked inside the wrecked car again. The injured man was trying to speak. Mark could hear him through the broken glass of the driver's window.

'Don't try to talk. Help is coming,' Mark said. 'You'll soon be out of there.'

There was blood on the man's face. He looked about the same age as Mark himself – somewhere in his mid-thirties.

'Julie,' the man said.

'Julian? Is that your name?'

'No! Please tell *Julie*,' the man said slowly. It was difficult for him to breathe. 'Tell her I'm sorry. I've been so stupid. Tell her, will you? Please tell Julie I'm sorry.'

'Your wife?'

'Yes, Julie, my wife,' the injured man said. 'I want her to know the truth.'

'The truth about what?' Mark asked.

The man coughed. Blood came from his mouth and ran down his face. In a moment, he was unconscious.

———

The ambulance and the fire engine arrived together. They stopped beside the wreckage of the Escort, their blue lights flashing. The fire crew began cutting at the wreckage and pulling away bits of torn and twisted metal. In a few minutes, they had removed part of the side of the car. Soon, two paramedics were beside the injured driver, trying to get him out of the wreck. As they worked, they spoke quietly to each other.

A police car arrived a minute later. Two officers got out. The male driver walked over to the wreck, and the other officer

– a woman – came to talk to Mark. He briefly described what he had seen to the young policewoman.

'Was he going fast?' she asked him.

'Yes, too fast, I suppose,' Mark said. 'And the road is icy here, on the bend. He just spun round and lost control. His car rolled over and over. I was fairly close behind him. I suppose I was going too fast too. It's lucky I didn't crash into him.'

At that moment, the paramedics managed to get the driver out of the wrecked car. They lifted him carefully and laid him on a stretcher on the ground. The man groaned once more, than he was silent.

Mark and the policewoman moved closer to them. One of the paramedics looked up. He shook his head.

'He's gone – there was no hope,' he said quietly.

Mark looked at the dead body on the stretcher. He felt both sad and angry. He realized he was trembling. The man's death had shocked him. It seemed so unnecessary. Somewhere the man's wife – Julie – was waiting for him, not knowing what had happened. And perhaps they had children.

The paramedics put the body in the back of the ambulance.

'Come to the car, sir,' the policewoman said to Mark. She took him by the arm.

They sat inside the police car. Mark told the policewoman again about everything that he had seen, and gave her his name and address. She wrote his words down in her notebook.

Soon the ambulance was ready to leave. The paramedics closed the back doors and climbed into the front seats. The ambulance drove away slowly.

The other officer returned to the police car. He sat in the driver's seat. He spoke quietly to his colleague. 'A breakdown truck[4] is coming to take away the wreckage,' he said. Then he turned and spoke to Mark. 'You look a bit pale, sir. Are you all right to continue your journey?'

'Yes, I'm fine,' Mark said. He was silent for a moment, then he added, 'I need to speak to that poor man's wife.'

'Don't worry, sir,' the policewoman said. 'We'll take care of that.'

Mark thought about the driver's wife getting a visit from the police late at night. He tried to imagine how she would feel.

'Yes, of course,' he said slowly. 'But I was the last person to speak to the man. I saw the accident happen. If his wife knows how the accident happened, perhaps it will help her. Can you give me the man's name and address?'

'We can't do that, sir,' the policeman said. 'The man's relatives will have to identify[4] the body first.'

'But I *must* speak to his wife,' Mark said. 'Before he died, he gave me a message for her. It was important to him, and it might help his wife accept his death.'

The policewoman spoke quietly to her colleague. 'He could phone me in a few days,' she said. 'The identification will have been made by then.'

The policeman nodded. 'OK,' he said.

The woman wrote down her name and phone number and gave it to Mark. 'You can get in touch with me at this number on Monday morning. I should be able to tell you the man's name and address then.'

Mark folded the piece of paper and put it inside his wallet. 'Thanks,' he said.

'We'll need you to call at the police station in Thame in the next day or two, sir,' the policewoman said. 'You were the only witness to the accident. We'll need you to sign a statement[4]. You'll probably have to attend the inquest[4] too.'

'Yes, of course,' said Mark. 'I'd better go now.'

'OK, sir,' the policewoman said. 'Drive carefully.'

As Mark drove away, he saw a breakdown truck approaching.

6

The News

While her husband was dying on an icy road in Oxfordshire, Julie Fenton was in her comfortable home in the city of Bath. She was sitting in the living-room with a magazine in her hands. Music was playing quietly on the stereo. Listening to music was Julie's way of relaxing. She had tried to interest Colin in classical music, but Colin always preferred blues and jazz.

Julie wasn't reading the magazine she was holding, and this evening the music didn't help her relax. She was worrying about a technical problem that she'd been having with the new software for Jackman's. And she was angry with her husband.

Colin had said that he would phone her from his hotel in Manchester. It was typical of him that he'd forgotten. No doubt, when he came home again in a few days' time, he'd have a good excuse for not phoning. He usually had good excuses.

At half past eleven, Julie yawned and put her magazine down. She looked at the phone, hoping it would ring, but it didn't. She switched off the stereo and went to bed.

In Brentwood, Linda and John Bentley were getting nervous. They sat quietly, listening to the sound of the kitchen clock ticking.

John had everything ready for the robbery. He was wearing black clothes and in his jacket pocket was a gun. On the chair next to him, there was a sports bag with some equipment inside. Suddenly, he stood up and started to walk nervously round the room.

'What's happened? Why hasn't Fenton phoned?' he said.

'Don't worry. He's been delayed, that's all,' Linda said.

John sat down again. He looked at the clock. It was now almost midnight. The agreed time for Colin's phone call had been eleven-thirty. Soon it would be time for them to leave for Sandwell's.

They heard a car stop outside the house. John lifted a curtain and looked through the window into the dark street. Immediately, he let the curtain fall again and stood back from the window.

'It's the police!' he said. 'What's that guy done, Linda? What's his game? Has he told the police about our plan?'

'Go upstairs,' Linda said. 'Keep out of the way. We've done nothing wrong. There's nothing to worry about.'

John grabbed his sports bag and ran upstairs. He hid in the bedroom at the back of the house.

A moment later, the doorbell rang. Linda went to the front door and opened it. Two police officers were standing in the doorway. One of the officers was a woman.

'Mrs Bentley?' the policewoman said.

'Yes.'

'We're very sorry to disturb[4] you at this time of night, but —'

The policewoman was silent for a moment. 'I'm sorry,' she went on. 'May we come in?'

'Yes, of course.'

They went into the living-room and sat down.

'It's about your husband, Mrs Bentley,' the policewoman said. 'I'm afraid he's had an accident.'

Linda opened her mouth, but no words came out. The policewoman touched her hand.

'I'm very sorry, Mrs Bentley,' the policewoman said, 'but your husband died earlier this evening. His car crashed on an icy road near Thame, in Oxfordshire.'

'I'm very sorry, Mrs Bentley, but your husband died earlier this evening.'

Linda looked down at the floor. This was terrible news. She'd never imagined that this could happen! She heard the policewoman say, 'I'm afraid you'll have to identify your husband's body.'

'Yes, of course,' Linda said, looking up at last.

'A police car will collect you tomorrow morning, at ten o'clock.'

When the police had gone, John came downstairs. Linda was in the kitchen making tea. She poured the boiling water into the pot. John stood in the doorway.

'Well?' he said. 'What did they want?'

'It's Colin,' she said. 'He's had a car accident. He's dead.'

'What did you tell the police?' John asked.

'Nothing,' Linda said. 'What *could* I tell them?'

'What happens now?' John asked.

'Be quiet! I must think,' Linda replied.

———

A few minutes later, Linda was calm again. She poured the tea into two mugs and put them on the table. She sat down next to her husband.

'Everything's changed now, John,' she said. 'But it's *good*. Everyone will think *you're* dead, not Colin Fenton. We've got to make sure that they go on thinking that.'

'We can't do that!' John said. 'The police will find out. And what about Fenton's wife? She'll soon start looking for him.'

'But she won't find him, will she?' Linda said. 'There'll be a funeral[4] in this area for someone called John Bentley. Why would anybody connect[4] *that* with the disappearance from Bath of a man called Fenton?'

'What about me?'

'You'll have to stay hidden for a while,' Linda replied. 'Then, when the funeral is over and everything's quiet again,

41

you'll do the robbery just as we planned. After that, we'll get away to Spain. It'll be all right, you'll see.'

They drank their tea in silence. Then Linda said, 'Tomorrow I'm going to be busy. The police are coming to collect me at ten o'clock. I've got to go to Oxford to identify "your" body! All you have to do is keep quiet in here. You'll have to stay in the back bedroom, with the curtains closed. If anyone sees or hears you, we're finished. Is that clear?'

'This is madness,' John said.

'Just do as I say, John, and everything will be all right,' Linda said again.

7
The Wife

When Mark Ashwood got home to his small house in Stratford-upon-Avon, he was exhausted. It was nearly one o'clock in the morning. Mark had had a long, tiring day.

Mark was an accountant and business consultant. He helped other business people with their tax problems, and gave small companies advice on how to improve their profits[1] and save money. That day, he had been to London to see a new client who owned a small clothing factory, and who wanted advice on exporting his products. Mark didn't know a lot about exporting, but he couldn't refuse an important new client. He would have to learn more about the export regulations[1] before his next meeting with the man.

Mark quickly ate some bread and cheese, then he went upstairs. One of the two bedrooms in his house was furnished as an office. He switched on the desk-lamp and sat down. His desk was tidy, as always. Pens and pencils were standing in a plastic holder. Mark pulled his copies of the Department of Trade and Industry's export regulations from a bookshelf.

Although it was late, he began to look through the thick books. He tried to concentrate, but he couldn't stop thinking about the man who had died earlier in the evening. 'Tell Julie I'm sorry,' the man had said. Mark didn't like the idea much, but he knew that he would have to visit Julie. He knew that he would have to carry out the dying man's last wish.

The following afternoon, Julie Fenton was working in her office in Bath when she had a phone call from Manchester. Jim Slater, at Jackman's, was wondering where Colin was. He had not appeared for their meeting that morning. Did Julie know if anything was wrong?

Julie was embarrassed. 'I'm sorry,' she told Slater. 'My husband left for Manchester yesterday. I can't think why he hasn't arrived. He may have been delayed at another client's office, but I'm sure he would have phoned you.'

'Well, as soon as you hear from him, please ask him to contact me,' Slater said.

'Of course,' Julie replied.

She put the phone down. She was furious. What did Colin think he was doing? Jackman's were such important clients.

Julie dialled the number of Colin's mobile phone, but she couldn't make contact. Colin had probably switched the phone off, she thought.

There was no news of Colin for the rest of the afternoon. Julie worked in the office until six-thirty, testing a new computer program that she was writing. She tried calling Colin's mobile phone several times more, but she could never make contact.

'Where the hell is he[3]?' Julie said to herself.

As Julie turned off her computer, Maggie, the company's secretary, was putting her coat on and getting ready to leave the office.

'I hope Colin's all right,' she said. 'It's strange that he hasn't called.'

'Perhaps I should phone his hotel,' Julie replied. 'It's past six-thirty now, he may have returned to his room. What's the hotel number, Maggie?'

Maggie looked a little embarrassed.

'I'm afraid I don't know which hotel Colin's staying at,' she said. 'Normally he asks me to make his hotel reservations for him, but this time he said he had already done it himself. I didn't think to ask him which hotel it was.'

'I'm afraid I don't know which hotel Colin's staying at,'
Maggie said.

'Well, we'll just have to wait for him to contact us then,' Julie said.

She was tired now as well as angry. It was typical of Colin to be so thoughtless. She switched off her desk-lamp and put on her coat.

'I've done enough for one day,' she said to Maggie. 'I'm going home too.'

———

As the evening passed, Julie's anger changed to worry and then to fear. Colin still hadn't got in touch. Julie began to think that something terrible might have happened. She went to bed but she slept badly, expecting the telephone to ring at any time. But the phone didn't ring.

In the morning, she got up feeling tired and miserable. She had to do something. She picked up the telephone and dialled the local police station.

'Good morning,' she said. 'I want to report a missing person.'

Half an hour later, a police car drove up to the house. Julie opened the front door and took the two officers – a woman and a young man – into the living-room.

'When exactly did your husband go missing[3], Mrs Fenton?' the policeman asked, as they all sat down.

'He went away on a business trip two days ago,' Julie began. 'But he failed to appear at the meeting he'd arranged, and I haven't heard from him at all since he left. I'm very worried about him.'

'Of course,' said the policeman. 'Does your husband often travel on business?'

'Yes, he goes away about once a month.'

'Has he ever failed to come home before?'

Julie hesitated. 'No,' she said finally.

'You don't seem certain.'

46

'Well, there have been a couple of times when he has stayed away from home,' Julie said. 'But those times were different – we had had arguments and he was angry with me. But he didn't stay away long. And he never missed business meetings.'

'I see,' the policeman said. 'And when was the last time this happened, Mrs Fenton?'

'About three years ago.'

'And there was no argument this time?'

'No,' Julie said.

The police officers asked for Colin Fenton's personal details – his age, his description, what clothes he had been wearing when Julie had last seen him. And they asked what type of car he drove and its registration number.

Julie took the police officers to the front door.

'We'll tell you if we hear anything, of course,' the police-woman said. 'But I must warn you, Mrs Fenton. If your husband doesn't want to return, that's not a matter for the police. If he has abandoned[4] you, that isn't a crime. The police can do nothing to help you.'

'I understand that,' Julie answered.

The police officers walked back to their car and Julie closed the door. She felt miserable and alone. She went to the kitchen and made a drink. Then she had a shower and put on fresh clothes, ready to go to the office. It was going to be another busy day.

8

The Funeral

It was late afternoon. John Bentley lay on the bed in the semi-darkness. Alone in the back bedroom of the house in Brentwood, and unable to leave it, he had plenty of time to think about what had happened. He and Linda were in big trouble, it seemed to him. He had no identity now, and he was a prisoner in his own home.

He tried to imagine his future, but he couldn't find anything to believe in. He had slept most of the earlier part of the day. But his sleep had been troubled by bad dreams and he had been woken from time to time by the ringing of the telephone. But now he was wide awake, waiting for Linda to return. She had gone to identify the body of her 'husband' and then to make arrangements for his funeral.

At last, John could lie still no longer. He went carefully downstairs to the kitchen and made himself a drink. He was still there at five-thirty when Linda came home. She was carrying Colin Fenton's suitcase. She was furious when she saw John in the kitchen.

'What are you doing down here?' she whispered angrily. 'Get upstairs at once.'

'I've not made any noise, Linda,' John said quietly. 'And I've not turned the light on.' He pointed at the kitchen curtains, which were closed. 'No one can see in.'

She let him stay.

'OK, sit on the floor,' Linda said. 'We can't take any risks.'

John did as he was told. He didn't want to go back upstairs yet. Linda checked the curtains carefully and switched on the electric light. Then she opened Colin Fenton's suitcase.

Inside the case, in a large plastic bag, were the clothes which Colin had been wearing when he died – he would be dressed in his business suit for his funeral. There were also some clean shirts and underclothes and a briefcase in the suitcase. In a smaller plastic bag there were a few personal items – Colin's watch, his wedding ring, and his mobile phone. The phone was broken. It had been in Colin's jacket pocket and it had been crushed by the steering wheel in the accident. The watch was broken too.

Linda threw the phone and the watch in the waste bin. She examined the ring carefully.

'It isn't worth much,' she said. 'But it *is* gold. I'll sell it later.' She put it inside her handbag.

Then she opened the dead man's briefcase. She glanced quickly at the papers and files inside it, then she threw those in the bin. There were several zipped pockets inside the briefcase. Linda checked them all, but she didn't find what she was looking for. She frowned.

'The police would have told me —' she began.

Then she stopped and checked the suitcase again. There was a zipped pocket inside that too. Linda opened it quickly. The envelope was still there! She pulled it out, opened it and counted the money nervously. £5000 – it was all there! She sighed. The money had been borrowed – it was part of an advance paid by Frankie Simpson for the jewellery he was going to fence for them.

'How are you feeling, John?' Linda asked her husband. She was calmer now.

'I need to get out of this house soon,' he replied. 'And the phone's been ringing all day.'

'I can believe that,' Linda said. Earlier that day, before going to identify the body, Linda had told the manager at the jewellery shop about John's 'death'. She had also told Frankie

Simpson about it, and Frankie would have told John's old friends at the *Red Lion*. People had obviously been phoning to talk to Linda about John's accident and to sympathize[4] with her. Well, she and John *had* to continue with the lie now. And anyway, only by doing that could they carry out the robbery and escape safely with the money.

'I'm hungry, Linda,' John said. 'I need something to eat.'

'You'd better get back upstairs,' she told him. 'I'll cook you something and bring it up to you in half an hour.'

John returned quietly to the back bedroom. He lay on the bed again, still angry with Linda for getting him into this situation. Soon he heard her coming upstairs. She entered the room carrying a tray with a plate of hamburgers on it. John sat up and he began to eat hungrily.

'I'm going out again now,' Linda said. 'I'll probably be back late.'

'Where are you going?' John did not want to be alone again.

'I'm going to get rid of[3] Fenton's car.'

Colin's BMW was in the Bentley's garage. Linda looked up and down the street before she went to get it. But it was dark outside now. The neighbours would not notice Linda driving away in a car which did not belong to her.

———

Linda drove to the M25, and travelled along it until she was on the western side of London. She turned off the motorway when she came to the exit for Heathrow Airport. She drove Colin's car into one of the long-stay car-parks and parked it there.

The long-stay car-park was a good place to leave Colin's car, Linda thought. It would be some time before anybody realized that the BMW had been abandoned. And when the police *did* know about it, they would think that Colin had got on a plane and left the country. They wouldn't search for him. They certainly wouldn't suspect that he was dead. Linda knew that hundreds of people went missing every year in Britain. Colin Fenton would simply become another missing person.

Linda walked from the car-park to Heathrow Central Underground station. Soon she was sitting on a train going back across the city. It was nearly midnight when she arrived at Upminster station. From there, she took a taxi home. John was asleep. The tray and the dirty plate were on the floor beside his bed.

———

The next few days were difficult for Linda. She couldn't stop visitors coming to the house. John had to stay inside his room most of the time and be very quiet. He felt like a trapped animal. Often, he wanted to run outside and scream, but he knew he had to stay hidden. He kept his gun in a drawer beside the bed. And sometimes, he took the gun out and held it in his hand. He'd never fired the gun at anyone. But as he lay there in the dark room, he wondered what it would be like to kill someone with it. After the first couple of days, he slept with the gun under his pillow. The gun made him feel safe.

Then it was the day of the funeral. The body was going to be cremated. Linda told everyone that that was what her husband had wanted. The funeral took place at a crematorium near Brentwood. A few of John and Linda's colleagues from Sandwell's came to the crematorium and so did Frankie Simpson and some of John's other mates from the Red Lion.

By the afternoon, all that was left of Colin Fenton was a container of ashes. Linda had asked for the ashes to be scattered in the garden of the crematorium.

———

When Linda arrived home after the cremation, she went upstairs to see how John was. She opened the door of the back bedroom. It was dark in the room, but Linda could just see her husband. He was pointing his gun at her.

51

A few of John and Linda's colleagues from Sandwell's came to the crematorium and so did Frankie Simpson.

'I've had enough of this, Linda,' he said angrily. 'I can't stay here any more. You've made me a prisoner.'

'You're not a prisoner, John,' she said calmly, as though talking to a child. She moved closer to him. 'We're in this together, John. We both have to be strong.'

'It's madness!' John said, sitting up. He was staring at Linda, furious with her. 'This whole plan is madness! It'll never work.'

Linda touched him gently on the arm. He pushed her hand away violently. 'Why have you done this to me?' he said. 'You've taken my life away from me. I'm trapped.'

'John,' she said softly, 'we've got to be patient. We need to wait just a couple of weeks, that's all. Then we'll do the robbery and we'll get away. No one will ever find us. And we'll have all the money we could want. Two more weeks and we'll be free, John. We'll be free forever.'

John allowed Linda to touch his arm now. 'I don't believe it,' he said quietly.

'You have to believe it, John,' Linda said. 'It's true.'

She sat on the bed beside him and she took the gun from his hand. 'Listen, John – in a few days' time, I'll go back to work. But I'm going to tell Mr Rose that I'll be leaving my job at Sandwell's at the end of the month. That's in just a couple of weeks. I'll tell him I can't live here alone, without my husband. I'll tell him I'm going back to Scotland. I've already cancelled the lease on this house. Just before I leave the shop, you'll do the robbery as we planned. Now that you're officially dead[4], your alibi is even better than before, isn't it? John Bentley can't rob shops – he's a dead man! It's the best possible alibi! And I'll only have to behave normally at work for a few days after the robbery.'

Suddenly, Linda smiled.

'I'm sorry John, my love,' she said. 'I know this is very difficult for you. Look, it's dark now. Let's go out for a couple of hours. We'll go for a drink and a meal. We'll go somewhere where nobody knows us. Let's go north towards Saffron Walden. We'll find a village pub in that area. Nobody will recognize you there.'

John realized that he had no choice but to agree to his wife's plan for the robbery. And after that, they would both have to leave the country as soon as possible. Meanwhile, he was happy with the idea of leaving the house for a few hours.

Ten minutes later, Linda was driving the van northwards, towards Cambridge. John was hiding in the back.

In a small village, just south of Saffron Walden, they stopped for a drink and a meal in an old pub. They weren't worried that anybody would know them there. It wasn't the kind of place their friends visited. As they sat in the warm restaurant, looking at the bright log fire, Linda put her hand on her husband's arm.

'Just a few weeks more, John,' she said again. 'Then we'll be free.'

9

The Advertisement

On the day her husband was cremated near Brentwood as 'John Bentley', Julie went to work early. She was in her office at C.J.F. Software Solutions before anyone else arrived. At nine o'clock, she moved from her own desk to Colin's. There was work to do – Colin's as well as her own – and she had a pile of letters and papers in front of her. She was trying to read them calmly and she was trying not to cry. But she couldn't stop the tears running down her cheeks. There had been no news of Colin and she was desperately worried.

Julie wasn't used to working on the company's finances. But the accounts had to be brought up to date, so she was trying to learn about them quickly. She read through the letters and she quickly filed the invoices, getting them ready to take to Mr Booker, the company's accountant.

Among the papers on the desk was a fax from Jackman's, the insurance brokers. It didn't contain good news. Jackman's didn't want to continue with the tests for the new software product. They'd decided that they were going to continue to use the software they already had. Julie was angry about this news. She'd wasted two months' development work on that project.

She pushed her fingers through her thick, red hair. Then she stood up and began walking round the room. She was tense. She needed time to relax and to think about the future of the business.

When Rob and Jenny – Julie's two assistant programmers – arrived at nine-thirty, she gave them a list of jobs to do during the day. Then she put the files of invoices into her briefcase and went to see Mr Booker.

Booker's office was dark and uncomfortably warm. Booker was sitting at his desk, his head down, his shoulders bent. When Julie entered the room, he spoke without looking up.

'I'm not surprised he's run away.'

'How did you know?' Julie said, sitting down in front of the desk. She had only met Booker once or twice before, but she didn't like him very much.

Booker coughed into his handkerchief. 'News like that travels fast,' he said slowly. 'It doesn't surprise me at all.'

'Why? What do you mean?'

'When I last saw your husband, we talked about your company's serious financial problems,' Booker replied. Julie looked puzzled[4]. 'He must have told you about our conversation,' Booker said.

'No,' Julie said. 'He told me nothing.'

Booker raised his eyebrows. 'Well, the simple truth is, you're spending more money than you're earning. Your company is seriously in debt.'

Julie looked straight at Booker, unable to believe what she was hearing. How could Colin have kept this news from her?

'How much do we owe?' she asked.

'About £10,000 at this moment,' Booker replied. 'Your husband said he'd arranged a bank loan. He was waiting for a valuable contract to be confirmed[1], and he needed the loan till you'd been paid for the new software.' Booker paused a moment. Then he said, 'That contract has been confirmed, hasn't it?'

Julie was shocked, but she was beginning to understand.

'No,' she said. 'It hasn't been confirmed. In fact, we've lost the contract.'

'I see,' Booker said. He smiled nastily. He seemed pleased. 'That explains everything then.'

'What do you mean?'

'Your husband can't accept failure, so he's run away.'

Julie didn't like what Booker was saying, or the unpleasant way he was saying it. She wondered why she and Colin had ever given him their accounts to work on. But she had no time to look for a new accountant now. She had enough problems already. She tried to be polite.

'My husband wouldn't run away. He is not that kind of person, Mr Booker,' she said. 'And anyway, he couldn't have known about the contract when he disappeared. I only had the news this morning.'

Julie put the folder of invoices on Booker's desk and got up to leave.

'You've got a big debt to pay back,' Booker said, lifting his head slightly. 'I'd do something about that very soon, if I were you.'

––––

That evening, Julie sat down at her kitchen table to do some more work on the company's finances. When she was too tired to continue, she made herself a hot drink, then went into the living-room. Some CD boxes lay in an untidy pile on the floor in front of the stereo. She picked one at random[4] and put it into the machine. A blues song started to play. Suddenly, tears were running down Julie's face again.

'Oh, Colin where are you?' she said aloud.

A photo of Colin stood on the low table beside the sofa. Julie picked it up. Colin, relaxed and smiling in the bright sunlight, was sitting outside a café by the sea. Julie had taken the photo herself two years before, while they were on holiday in the south of France. She shook her head as the tears ran down her cheeks.

'Where are you?' she repeated in a soft voice.

She could no longer keep the bad thoughts out of her mind. Perhaps the police were right. Perhaps Colin *had* abandoned her because he didn't love her any more. Or perhaps *Booker* was right, and Colin had run away from his business problems because he couldn't accept failure. Julie didn't know who was right. And she didn't care. All she wanted was to have her husband back home again.

'Somebody, somewhere must know where Colin is,' she thought. 'Somebody must have seen him!'

She decided to put an advertisement in the national newspapers. She would put Colin's photo in the ad. Someone might remember seeing him. Someone might help her find him again.

'Somebody, somewhere must know where Colin is.'

10

The Search

Mark Ashwood switched off his computer. He put some papers into a folder and he put the folder on a shelf. The research on export regulations which he'd done for his new client had been interesting. Now he'd finished preparing a report on what he'd learnt. He went downstairs and got himself a cold drink from his fridge. It was a Friday evening, and Mark had finished work for the week.

On the Monday morning after the car accident, he had telephoned the policewoman at Thame, and he'd learnt the identity and the address of the man who had died. But for the next couple of weeks, Mark had been too busy to think about a visit to the man's wife, or about what he might say to her.

Mark finished his drink and sighed happily. He had arranged to go out with some friends that evening. And the next day they were all going climbing in Wales. In Mark's opinion, rock-climbing was the perfect way to relax. It was a sport that required calmness and self-control[4]. And it was exciting to climb a steep rock face with nothing below you but the sea.

He was going to enjoy his weekend. But on Monday, he'd take the report to his new client in east London, and then – he decided – he'd better visit Mrs Bentley. She was the widow of the man who had died in the crash. He had to tell her what her husband had said just before his death.

Mark set off from Stratford-upon-Avon early on the Monday morning. He reached his new client's offices on the south-east side of London just before ten-thirty. Mark and his client spent

the rest of the morning, and the whole of the afternoon, discussing exports and other business. When their discussions
were completed, Mark and his client made arrangements for
another meeting in about ten days' time.

A few minutes later, Mark was sitting in his blue Volvo in
the company's car-park, studying a map of the Brentwood area.
Having found John Bentley's street on the map, he started his
car and drove towards Brentwood. He'd decided not to phone
the man's widow first. It would be difficult to tell her that he
wanted to visit her, without telling her why. And he didn't
want to tell her *that* till he *saw* her.

It was dark now, and it was raining. People were leaving
their work-places and going home, so the roads were very busy.
It was an hour before Mark reached the address he was looking
for.

Mark parked his car outside the Bentley's house. The street
was long and straight, and it was lined on both sides with small
square houses with garages beside them. The street was not
well lit.

Mark switched off his car engine and looked up at the
house. There were no lights burning inside. It looked as though
Mrs Bentley wasn't at home. Mark's journey had probably been
a waste of time.

He hurried to the front door and rang the bell. To his surprise, he heard sounds of movement inside the house. And for
a moment, he saw a light through the glass in the front door –
a light in a back room of the house. Someone was at home
after all! He rang the bell again. Then the light in the back
room went off. Now the house seemed silent and empty.

Mark went back to his car and wondered what to do. He was
going to visit his client in London again in about ten days'
time. He could try to contact Mrs Bentley again then. But he
really wanted to see her at once. He'd prepared carefully what

he wanted to say, and he wanted to say it today!

He glanced at his watch. It was a quarter to seven. Mark decided to go and eat some dinner somewhere and then to come back. If Julie wasn't home when he returned, he'd have to try again the next time he was in London. He started the engine, and drove away to find a pub or a restaurant.

———

That afternoon, Linda Bentley had told the manager at Sandwell's that she wanted to leave her job at the end of the month. Mr Rose liked Linda, and he was sorry to hear her news. But he hadn't argued with her. He hadn't tried to change her mind.

As soon as the shop closed, Linda went to see Frankie Simpson at the Red Lion. She'd telephoned first, and Frankie was expecting her when she arrived at six-thirty that evening. They sat together at a table in the corner of the pub.

'Shall we get down to business[3]?' Frankie said. 'You told me that the deal[1] we arranged will still go ahead.'

'Yes,' Linda replied. 'John's death makes no difference to the deal.'

'And you want me to fence a big pile of jewellery. Is that right?'

'Yes. More than one million pounds' worth.'

Frankie raised his eyebrows. 'That's a hell of a lot[3] of jewellery, Linda,' he said.

'Can you sell the jewellery for me?'

'Yes, I can fence it,' Frankie said. 'But who's going to do the robbery? I thought John was going to do it, but now —'

'You don't need to know that,' Linda replied. 'When will I get the cash?'

'It isn't easy to raise that much cash[1],' Frankie said. 'I can't fence that much jewellery in the London area. Some of it'll have to go north, to Birmingham and to Manchester. I've got good contacts in the jewellery trade[4] in both cities, but it'll take a little time to move the stuff.'

'So how long *will* it take?'

'It would help if I knew exactly what kind of stuff you're going to bring me,' Frankie said.

'I can give you a detailed list,' Linda said. 'I'll let you have it in a few days.'

'When's the robbery going to happen?'

'In about ten days' time.'

Frankie thought for a moment. Then he said, 'As soon as I get that list, I can inform my contacts. That way, I'll make sure they'll have the cash ready when we deliver the jewellery. Of course, these people won't pay more that fifty per cent of the jewellery's value. You know that, don't you?'

'Yes, I know that, Frankie.'

'OK, well, give me three days after you hand over the stuff to me. Then you'll be able to collect the cash.'

'Fine,' Linda said.

'And while we're talking about money, we'd better discuss my share, Linda,' Frankie said. 'Fencing stolen jewellery is a dangerous business. I'll be taking a big risk. What are you offering me?'

'Seventy-five thousand pounds,' Linda said.

Frankie laughed. 'That's not enough, my dear,' he said. 'There's a big risk, and I'll need a lot of help. I'll have to pay my men.'

'How much do you want then?'

'A hundred and twenty thousand.'

It was Linda's turn to laugh. 'You must be joking,' she said.

'We've got to move the stuff fast,' said Frankie. 'And that costs money.'

'OK. I'll give you one hundred thousand – no more,' said Linda.

'Okay, Linda,' Frankie agreed. 'It's a deal.'

It was nine o'clock that evening when Linda turned onto the drive in front of her garage. The headlights of her van lit up the figure of a man standing at her front door. Linda got out of the van and went up to him.

'Who are you?' she said. 'What do you want?'

'Mrs Bentley?' Mark asked.

'Yes.'

'I'm very sorry to call so late, but I was in the area and I need to speak to you. My name's Ashwood – Mark Ashwood.'

Linda looked puzzled. They stood there in the dark, staring at each other.

'You don't know me,' Mark went on. 'I've got to talk to you about your husband, Mrs Bentley. I was there when he died. He asked me to give you a message.'

Linda unlocked the front door. 'Come in,' she said.

As they stepped into the house, a voice called out, 'Linda, is that you?'

Linda stopped suddenly. For a moment, Mark saw a figure at the top of the stairs. But almost at once the man turned and disappeared into one of the upstairs rooms. Suddenly, Mark's body was trembling with shock, as though he'd seen a ghost! The man's face had been exactly like the face of John Bentley, the man he'd seen die near Thame.

Linda had to think quickly, but that was something that she'd always been good at. She smiled sadly at Mark.

'A dear friend of mine is keeping me company,' she said. 'And my friend wasn't expecting me to arrive home with anybody else. And as my husband died so recently —' She shrugged her shoulders. 'Well, it doesn't look good to have a man in the house, does it?'

Mark didn't know what to say. He felt foolish and he wished

For a moment, Mark saw a figure at the top of the stairs.

he hadn't come.

'I'm sorry, Mrs Bentley,' he said nervously.

'Come into the living-room,' Linda said. 'I'll make us some tea.'

Mark sat down in the Bentleys' living-room and listened to the sounds of the woman making tea in the kitchen. He was confused. What was happening here? The man in the wrecked car had given him a message for his wife, Julie. But the man at the top of the stairs had called out 'Linda' not 'Julie'.

Soon the woman came into the room carrying tea-things on a tray. She poured tea into two cups, and handed one to Mark.

'You must think I'm a terrible person,' she said. 'But the truth is, my husband and I weren't very happy together. Perhaps you understand? Are you married yourself?'

'No, I'm not,' Mark said, sipping his tea. It was time to say what he had come here to say. 'Your husband was driving in front of me that night, Mrs Bentley,' he went on. 'The road was covered in ice. I saw his car spin on the ice and crash into a tree. I stopped to help him. Before he died, he asked me to speak to you. I'm sure he said, "Tell Julie I'm sorry." Those were his last words. But if your name is Linda, not Julie, perhaps I misunderstood him.'

'Perhaps my husband was confused,' Linda said.

'Yes, perhaps he was,' said Mark.

'I'm glad you came, Mr Ashwood,' Linda said. 'It was very good of you to visit me.' She smiled. 'I appreciate⁴ what you did for my husband when he was dying.'

Mark finished his tea and stood up. 'I'd better go now,' he said.

The woman took him to the front door and watched him hurry down the dark path towards his car.

———

It was almost one o'clock when Mark arrived home in Stratford. He had a shower then he went to bed. But he couldn't sleep. He couldn't relax. His meeting with Mrs Bentley had worried him badly. Had the Bentleys' marriage really been so bad? It must have been, he thought. Only a few weeks after her husband's death, Mrs Bentley hadn't seemed unhappy. And she'd had another man in her house – a man who looked exactly like her dead husband. It was all very strange. And as John Bentley was dying, he had spoken about his wife, calling her Julie. But Mrs Bentley seemed to be called Linda, not Julie. That was strange too! There was a puzzle here and Mark wanted to solve it. He thought about these things for hours, until he finally fell asleep.

The next morning, he got up later than usual. He was tired after his restless night. He took his daily national newspaper from the letterbox, and went into his kitchen to make some breakfast. He read the newspaper while he ate.

For the second time in two days, he had a shock. On one of the inside pages, among the ads, there was a photo of a man whose face he immediately recognized. It was the man who had died in the car crash near Thame.

Above the photo were the words: *Have you seen this man?* Below it, there was a brief description: *Colin Fenton, 35, disappeared on the evening of 10th January. If you have any information about him, please phone Julie Fenton on 01522 35912.*

Had Mark now found the Julie he was looking for?

'There's certainly a puzzle here,' Mark thought. 'But perhaps I'm beginning to solve it.'

11

The Visit

On the morning that Julie Fenton's ad appeared in the newspapers, she didn't go to her office – she stayed at home, hoping for news. During the morning, two people phoned her. They both called to say that they thought they'd seen Colin on the day of his disappearance. They both thought they'd seen him at a service area on the M4 motorway, near Swindon. This information didn't help Julie much. She felt no closer to finding Colin.

Just before one o'clock, the phone rang again. It was a call from a police officer. Colin's car had been found at Heathrow Airport.

That afternoon, Julie went to collect the car. A police officer from Heathrow met her and took her to the BMW, which was in one of the long-stay car-parks. It was not damaged in any way.

'You say that you found nothing belonging to my husband inside the car?' Julie asked.

'Nothing, madam,' the officer replied.

Julie opened the driver's door and looked inside. Then she looked inside the boot.

'My husband had some luggage with him – a suitcase and a briefcase. Didn't you find those?'

'I'm afraid not, madam.'

'What was he doing here at Heathrow Airport?'

'I'm very sorry, madam,' the police officer said. 'We don't know. But we think that he probably got on a plane. Perhaps he wanted to leave the country? Did your husband have his passport with him?'

That evening, Julie looked in the drawer of Colin's bedside table. He usually kept his passport in the drawer. When she didn't find it, she wept tears of anger and grief. She didn't want to believe that Colin had abandoned her. She and Colin had had a difficult marriage. Colin had been irresponsible sometimes, and sometimes he'd been thoughtless. But he wasn't a cruel man.

Julie was sitting in the dark, too tired to switch on the light, when the phone rang. She felt for the phone and picked it up.

'Julie Fenton?' a man's voice asked.

'Yes.'

'My name's Ashwood – Mark Ashwood. I saw your ad in the newspaper. I believe I've got some information about your husband.'

Julie went cold. 'Do you know where he is?' she asked.

Mark was not sure how to answer. 'No, not exactly, Mrs Fenton,' he said. 'I'm sorry, but the news I have isn't good. I'd prefer to meet you and speak to you. Perhaps I could meet you tomorrow?'

Julie was suspicious. Why did this man want to meet her? What was stopping him giving her the information over the phone?

'If you're going to tell me that my husband has left the country, I already know that,' she said.

'I'm afraid you're wrong about that, Mrs Fenton,' the man said. 'But I won't say any more just now. I'd really like to tell you when I meet you. Although the information I have isn't good, I believe it will help you. Can I come and see you tomorrow?'

Julie wasn't happy about the man's request, but finally she agreed to meet him.

'All right,' she said. She gave him her address. 'What time can you be here?'

'Is ten-thirty OK?' the man asked.

'Yes, ten-thirty is fine,' Julie said.

'I'll see you tomorrow, then,' the man said. 'Goodbye.'

Julie put the phone down and switched on the light. She realized that she hadn't eaten that evening. She was confused and tired. After some hot tea and a little food, she tried to do some work at the kitchen table, but it was hopeless. Soon, she went up to bed.

———

The doorbell rang while Julie was still eating breakfast. She'd slept till nine o'clock, and she hadn't been downstairs long.

'Come into the kitchen,' she said to Mark. 'Let me give you some coffee. I'm having some myself.'

Mark followed her into the kitchen. The table was covered in papers where Julie had been working the previous evening. Julie moved the papers and took a mug from the cupboard. Mark saw that there was a pile of unwashed dishes in the sink.

Julie poured Mark's coffee and sat down at the table opposite him.

'Sorry about the mess,' she said. 'I woke late.'

Mark looked at her. Her eyes were tired, her skin was pale. He tried to think of how he should begin his story. 'This must be very difficult for you,' he said.

Julie sipped some coffee and nodded. 'You told me to be prepared for bad news,' she said. Mark was silent. 'I need to know what has happened, Mr Ashwood.'

'I'm afraid your husband is dead, Mrs Fenton,' Mark said slowly. He waited for a reaction[4], but there was none. 'It was an accident,' Mark went on. 'It was quite late in the evening, about ten o'clock. I was driving behind your husband along a narrow country road. He lost control of his car on some ice, and it crashed into a tree.'

'But why haven't I been informed?' Julie said. 'The police

would have told me if my husband had had an accident.'

'The police believed he was someone else,' Mark said. 'Someone called John Bentley.'

Julie laughed nervously. 'What *are* you talking about?' she said.

'For some reason, your husband was carrying John Bentley's documents,' said Mark.

Julie suddenly felt angry. This man seemed crazy.

'Where did this accident happen?' she asked.

'Not far from Thame, in Oxfordshire,' Mark replied. 'I'd been to London for the day and I was driving home to Stratford-upon-Avon.'

'Let me tell you something, Mr Ashwood,' Julie said. 'My husband's BMW was found undamaged in a car-park at Heathrow Airport yesterday. And you're telling me that he died in an accident! Please, don't waste my time.'

'It was a Ford Escort, not a BMW,' Mark said. 'He must have been driving someone else's car – probably John Bentley's.'

Julie laughed again. 'But why? This is crazy!'

'Listen, I realize that all this seems strange,' Mark said. 'That's why I didn't want to speak on the phone. But believe me, what I'm telling you is true.'

'I think you've made a terrible mistake, Mr Ashwood,' Julie said. 'Please don't bother me with any more silly stories. I'm a busy woman.'

'The man I saw die was your husband,' Mark said. 'I'm sure of that. He told me your name, Julie. "Tell Julie I'm sorry," he said to me.'

'The man who died must have been this John Bentley,' Julie said. 'Not my husband.'

'I thought so too, at first,' Mark said. 'So two days ago, I went to see John Bentley's wife. But her name wasn't Julie. It was Linda.'

'And her husband was alive and well, I suppose?'

Mark drank some of his coffee. 'No,' he quietly. He knew what the woman was going to say next.

'Ah! No doubt, he'd died in a car accident?' Julie said. She sighed deeply. 'I think you'd better go, Mr Ashwood.'

Mark stood up. 'I know that what I'm saying is a shock for you,' he said. 'But it's true. I'm sorry if I've made you unhappy. I had to come here and speak to you. Your husband asked me to come. It was his last wish.'

Suddenly Julie was crying. 'Please go now,' she said.

Mark took his business card from his wallet and put it on the table in front of Julie. 'I'll leave you my card,' he said. 'My phone number's on it. Think about what I've said. Please call me if you want to talk. I believe I can help.'

Julie didn't reply. She sat shaking her head, looking down at the floor and crying quietly. Mark left the house sadly.

'Your husband asked me to come. It was his last wish.'

12

The Robbery

After Mark Ashwood's unexpected visit to Brentwood, it was clear to the Bentleys that John couldn't stay hidden in the house any longer. Linda found a cheap hotel for him in a suburb which was nearer central London, not far from the River Thames. The hotel was the kind of place where you paid in advance for your room and nobody asked you any questions. It was an old building and some of the windows had boards over them. On the ground floor there was a small, ugly bar, where people in cheap clothes sat drinking all day. John's room on the first floor was dark and dirty. The glass in the window was cracked.

It was late on a Tuesday evening. John Bentley was excited and nervous. He and Linda sat in the cold hotel room, waiting. There was a bottle of whisky on the table beside the bed. John lifted the bottle to his lips and drank. For a few moments he felt calm. Then the nervous excitement returned. This was the night! After tonight, he would be free forever!

At one-fifteen in the morning, John checked his things – a set of keys, a small torch, a pair of rubber gloves, a roll of adhesive tape, a small wooden box, a car jack[4] and his gun. He put the keys, the gloves, the torch, the tape and the gun in his pockets, and he put the jack and the wooden container in his black sports bag.

'It's time to go,' he told Linda.

They got into the van and Linda drove it towards the centre of London. The city streets were quiet. It took about twenty minutes to reach Sandwell's.

The jewellery shop was a two-storey building. The front of the shop was in a wide, busy shopping street, but there was a back door too. This door was in a quiet road where delivery trucks stopped. In this road, apart from back doors of shops, there were some offices and a bank, but there were no houses. No one went there late at night. Linda drove the van to the back of Sandwell's. She and John checked their watches. It was one thirty-five.

'Come back in exactly half an hour,' John said. Then he got out of the van, carrying his sports bag, and he watched as Linda drove slowly away.

Standing in the shadow of the shop's back door, John pulled on his rubber gloves. He took the set of keys from his pocket and unlocked the steel shutter[4] that protected the door. Then he lifted the shutter and he used another key to open the door itself. Now he had twenty seconds to enter the correct code on the keypad of the shop's security system. If he failed, the alarm bells would ring, here and in the nearest police station.

John dropped his sports bag inside the door, then he took the torch from his pocket and turned it on. He ran along the corridor which led towards the front of the building. Half way along the corridor, on the right, was the door to the manager's office and on the wall outside this was the keypad. By the light from the torch, John quickly keyed in the six-figure code. Then he ran back along the corridor, pulled down the steel shutter, and locked it from the inside. Next, he closed and locked the door.

John stood with his back against the door, breathing hard, his heart beating fast. Now he was safe for a while. He waited for a few moments. Then he picked up his sports bag and walked towards the front of the building again.

The corridor led to the shop itself, and to the stairs which went up to the workshop on the upper storey. But half way along on the left, opposite Mr Rose's office door, was the door to the strong-room. In here, the shop's main stock[1] was kept, as well as some very valuable stones which would be made into special pieces of jewellery in the workshop.

Leaving his sports bag in the corridor, John turned to the door of the strong-room. It was a heavy steel door with an electronic combination lock. John keyed in the correct code, pushed the door open, and entered the room. There were no windows in the strong-room, so it would be safe to switch on the light. But first, John had to do something about the video camera which was fixed high on the wall above the door. Whenever the light was on inside the strong-room, the camera sent pictures to a video recorder in the manager's office.

John took off his coat and threw it over the camera, so that it covered the lens. Only then did he turn on the light. The strong-room was lined with shelves on three walls. Against the fourth wall, next to the door, was a steel cabinet with many drawers. Inside these drawers were the precious stones, as well as the most expensive pieces of jewellery that were displayed in the shop during the daytime. On the shelves around the strong-room were boxes of good-quality, but somewhat less expens ive pieces.

John removed the boxes and carried them to the back door, piling them neatly, one on top of another. Then he returned to the strong-room. In a corner, he found a large empty box. He put it on a table next to the steel cabinet, then he removed the top two drawers – the drawers containing precious stones – from the cabinet and carefully placed them inside the empty box. He added the trays of extremely valuable rings, necklaces and brooches from the lower draws. When the box was full, he took the roll of adhesive tape from his pocket, sealed the box and pulled it to the back door. Finally, he turned off the strong-room light, pulled his coat down from the camera, and went out

… he removed the drawers containing precious stones from the cabinet…

into the corridor, closing the door behind him.

He reset the lock and he took the wooden box from his bag. He opened it and took out a piece of plastic explosive[2], which he pressed onto the strong-room lock, together with a detonator. He used the tape to keep the detonator and its timer in place.

Next, John picked up his sports bag, removed the car jack, put the wooden box back in the bag and went into the front of the shop. He held his torch in his mouth and opened two glass display cabinets[4] with his keys. The cabinets contained some good pieces of jewellery, and he threw the contents into his bag. Finally, he relocked the cabinets and used the car jack to smash the glass. Then he took the sports bag to the back door and put it on the pile of boxes.

He checked his watch. It was five minutes to two. There was no time to lose. He had another ten minutes before Linda returned with the van.

John ran up the stairs to the workshop, holding the car jack in his hand. There was a skylight in the roof which was locked from the inside. And below the skylight was a grille of metal bars. John stood on a chair. He took his car jack, and pushed it between the two central bars of the grille. He turned the jack's long handle quickly, forcing the bars apart. Soon the gap between them was wide enough for a man to climb through. He removed the jack and used it to smash the skylight's glass and lock. He opened the skylight.

John hurried downstairs to the strong-room door, still carrying the jack. He checked his watch. It was five past two. Linda should arrive at any moment. He set the timer of the detonator and ran along the corridor. He leant against a wall and waited, breathing hard, wiping the sweat from his face with the back of his hand. After a minute, he heard a small explosion. He ran back to the strong-room door. The lock had been destroyed!

At that moment, he heard a van stop outside the back door of the shop. He unlocked and opened the door, then he unlocked and lifted the shutter. Linda had parked the van just outside, and had opened its back doors. John and Linda worked quickly, lifting the boxes from the corridor and sliding them into the back of the van. When they'd loaded the boxes, John threw in his jack and his sports bag. He closed the doors. Then he rushed back inside to the keypad and reset the alarm code while Linda started the van.

Immediately the alarm started ringing. The noise was terrible and it seemed to fill the empty street. John ran back outside, closed and locked the back door of the shop, pulled down the shutter and locked that. Then he jumped into the van, slamming the passenger's door behind him.

Linda drove away down the street at high speed, the tyres screaming as she turned the corner. But after a few minutes, she slowed down. Soon she was driving carefully towards the cheap hotel by the river. John got out of the van at the hotel, and Linda drove on till she came to the Red Lion.

Frankie Simpson was waiting for her at the pub. It was ten to three in the morning and there was nobody in the street. Frankie helped Linda to get the jewellery into the building. Then the two of them began to check the items of jewellery against the list that Linda had already given Frankie. It was a long job and it took them nearly two hours.

Linda kept some of the jewellery. A few pieces, she wanted to wear herself. The others she would sell later, when she and John had escaped to Spain. While Linda had a drink, Frankie Simpson began separating and repacking the jewellery, ready for his men to deliver to other fences in London, Birmingham and Manchester.

'Two days,' Frankie said. 'You'll have your money in two days. OK?'

'Right,' said Linda. 'I'll meet you here on Friday evening.'
'Come at around five o'clock,' Frankie said.
'I'll be here,' said Linda.

———

When Linda finally got home it was almost six o'clock. She went to bed for a while, but at seven-thirty she was up again. She had to go to work!

———

Linda arrived at Sandwell's at ten to nine, as she did every Monday to Friday. Two police cars were parked nearby. Linda walked into the shop, trying to look surprised. The other staff members were already there. They were standing together, talking. Uniformed police officers were examining the broken display cabinets. Mr Rose was talking to a police inspector who was wearing a raincoat.

Linda walked over to her colleagues.

'What's happened here?' she said, looking around the shop. 'And *when* did it happen?'

'We think some thieves got in through the skylight, in the middle of the night,' one of them replied. 'They smashed the glass and the lock and they forced open the bars of the grille.'

'Are there any clues that will help the police to identify the thieves?' Linda asked quietly.

'A well-organized gang – that's what the police think,' the colleague replied. 'There must have been several thieves, and they must have worked fast. They broke in at five past two – that's when the alarm bells started ringing – and they had gone when the police arrived at a quarter past two.'

The manager finished speaking to the police inspector. He came over to Linda and her colleagues.

'The police have asked us not to touch anything here until they have checked for fingerprints,' Mr Rose said. 'And they will talk to each of you to see if you know anything that might help them. Perhaps someone will make coffee for us all? I'll be in my office.'

One of the policemen came to talk to Linda. He asked if she had any ideas about who the thieves were. And he asked where she had been the previous evening. But Mr Rose had told the police officers that Linda's husband had recently died, and the man questioned her very gently. When she said that she had been alone at home the previous night, the officer thanked her politely and went on to talk to someone else.

Linda made lots of coffee. She gave some to her colleagues and to the police officers. Then she took a cup to the manager's office. Mr Rose was talking on the phone to the shop's insurance company. Linda put the coffee on his desk. She was about to leave the room when the manager finished his phone call.

'Linda, there's no need for you to stay here,' he said. 'The shop will be closed for a few days, I expect. Since you're leaving at the end of the week anyway, you might as well finish work now. I expect you have a lot to do before you move to Scotland.'

'That's very good of you, Mr Rose,' Linda said. 'I *am* very busy. There's a lot of packing and cleaning to do at the house.'

'Are you going back to Glasgow immediately?'

'Yes,' Linda replied. 'I've been lonely in London since John's death. I need to move away – the sooner the better.'

'Do you need any help?' the manager asked. 'I could send one of the others to help you, if you want.'

'No, I can manage,' Linda said. 'But thanks anyway.'

'We'll miss you,' Mr Rose said. 'We'll miss both of you – John was good man and a hard worker.'

Linda looked down for a moment. 'Yes,' she said.

A few minutes later, Linda left Sandwell's for the last time. She walked through the shop, stepping over pieces of broken glass, and out into the street.

13

The Truth

On the Thursday evening, despite being tired after a long day's work, Julie Fenton decided to do some housework. She began by picking up the newspapers and magazines which lay all over the house. Then she started to clean her bedroom. Unwashed clothes lay in a big pile on a chair. She washed them and dried them. Then she folded them and put them back on the chair, ready to iron.

In one of the drawers in the bedroom, Julie kept her personal documents – bank statements, receipts[4], her passport, etc. She wanted to check a couple of the bank statements. She pulled open the drawer, and she took out the documents to start sorting them. It was then that she saw something that gave her a bad shock. Under the pile of documents was Colin's passport! And if Colin's passport was in the drawer, then he *couldn't* have left the country. He couldn't have left the country without the passport. So he hadn't abandoned her. He must have had an accident. Perhaps he was lying ill, or unconscious, somewhere.

Julie sat down on the bed. Then she remembered what Mark Ashwood had told her. On the day of Colin's disappearance, Mark had been driving north near Thame when he had seen a fatal accident. That was at about ten-thirty p.m. Other people said they had seen Colin at a service area on the M4 earlier the same evening. What if Colin *had* been involved[4] with this John Bentley – the man that Mark Ashwood had talked about?

Julie realized she needed to speak to Mark Ashwood again. She hurried downstairs, hoping that she hadn't thrown away

Mark's business card. After a minute, she found it in the kitchen, among some letters that were lying on top of the fridge. She picked up the phone and called Mark's number immediately.

'This is Julie Fenton,' she said when Mark answered.

'I'm glad you phoned,' Mark said.

'I need to talk to you,' said Julie. 'I've thought about what you said. You could be right. Perhaps the man you saw die *was* my husband. I need to find out as much as possible about that man's death.'

'Perhaps it's better if we meet,' Mark said. 'Can you come to Stratford tomorrow?'

'Yes,' Julie said. 'I'm busy in the morning, but I can be with you by two-thirty, if that's OK?'

'That's fine,' Mark replied. 'The address is on my card.'

———

The following morning, Julie got up very early. She did about five hours' work before driving to Stratford-upon-Avon. It was a clear, cold, sunny day. The journey took about two hours.

Mark made some coffee. Then he and Julie sat in his living-room drinking from small china cups. Mark described the accident once more.

'Why do you think Colin had Bentley's documents, and why was he was driving Bentley's car?' she asked when Mark had finished speaking.

'I wish I knew,' Mark replied. 'I went to see Bentley's wife. Of course, I expected her to be called Julie. I felt foolish when I found out that her name was Linda. But that wasn't the only surprising thing. There was a man in the house. I only saw him for a moment, but he looked exactly like your husband.'

'What are you saying?' Julie exclaimed.

'Well, obviously it *wasn't* Colin,' Mark said.

'Then who was it?'

'It could have been John Bentley,' Mark said. 'I'm sure that he and your husband had exchanged identities on that day in January. I don't know why. But they were able to do it because they were doubles – they looked just like each other.'

There was a silence. Julie looked thoughtful. Then she said quietly, 'There must have been a funeral.'

'Yes, I suppose you're right. It won't be hard to find out if there was a funeral for someone called John Bentley in the Brentwood area in the weeks after the accident.'

Julie thought that there was something deeply wrong about all this. Colin had died, but there was no official record of his death. Someone else, some strange woman, had taken Colin from her, had given him a new name, and had had him buried or cremated.

'This is horrible, Mark!' she said.

'I'm sorry,' Mark said. 'I really am sorry.'

'I won't rest until I've given Colin back his own name,' Julie said. 'Will you help me?'

Mark looked at the sad woman who was sitting next to him.

'Yes, I'll help you,' he said. 'Let's go for a walk. It's a sunny day. We can talk some more and decide what to do next.'

The small town of Stratford was peaceful that afternoon. They walked along the banks of the River Avon. A woman and two children were throwing pieces of bread to the swans and ducks on the river.

Julie and Mark sat on a bench, looking at the river. There were huge willow trees on the far bank. In a few weeks' time, there would be new green leaves on them. There would be new life everywhere.

'It's time for *me* to start a new life too, Mark,' Julie said, looking at the trees. 'But first, I have to go and see this woman, this Linda Bentley. She's the only person who can give me the answers that I need before I can start my new life.'

84

'I'll come with you,' Mark said. 'I can take you to where she lives.'

'All right,' Julie said. 'But can we go now?'

Mark looked at his watch. It was quarter to four. If they left immediately, they could be in London by six or six-thirty.

'Come on then,' he said. 'We'll take my car.'

85

14

The Chase

While Mark and Julie were driving towards London, Linda Bentley was making preparations to leave her house. A large suitcase lay open in her bedroom. Linda was filling it with some clothes and some other personal belongings. All her other clothes, and everything else that she did not want to take with her, were in plastic bags outside the front door.

In her shoulder bag she put her own passport and her husband's too. The fact that John was officially dead wouldn't stop him travelling. Linda hadn't told the British Passport Authority[4] that he was dead, so he could still use his passport. And the border officials in France and Spain wouldn't know that he was officially dead, of course. Once they were in Spain, they could get themselves new identities and new documents.

By around three-thirty, Linda was ready to leave. But there was something she had to do first. She had to get her money from Frankie Simpson. She closed the suitcase and carried it downstairs to the hall.

She drove the van to the Red Lion. Frankie was waiting for her in an upstairs room. Linda sat down opposite him. Frankie pointed to a holdall by her chair. Linda opened it. It was full of banknotes.

'I've counted the money,' Frankie said. 'It's all in fifty-pound notes. They're in bundles of £5000.'

Linda quickly counted the bundles. 'Thanks, Frankie,' she said.

'If ever you need my help again,' Frankie went on, 'you know where to find me, Linda.'

Linda stood up. 'Yes. Thanks, Frankie,' she said. 'But this

'It's all in fifty-pound notes. They're in bundles of £5000.'

won't happen again. And you won't be seeing me any more.'

———

It was just before six o'clock when Linda arrived back at her house. A few minutes later, the owner of the house arrived to collect the keys. Linda brought her suitcase from the hall and put it in the van, next to the holdall. Then she closed the door of the house and put the keys into the owner's hand.

'Goodbye,' she said. 'And thank you.' She took one last look at the house, then she got in the van and started the engine. She didn't notice the blue car that had parked on the other side of the street a few seconds earlier.

———

Mark and Julie had arrived outside the Bentleys' house just in time to see Linda put a suitcase into her van, and give her house keys to a tall, thin man with a moustache.

'We're too late,' Mark said. 'She's leaving.'

'We must follow her, Mark,' Julie said. 'I must know where she's going. If we don't follow her now, I may never find her again.'

Mark turned his car round and drove after Linda's van. The streets were full of traffic and nobody was going very fast. Mark made sure he always kept the van in sight. And at first, Linda didn't notice that she was being followed. But half an hour later, when she arrived at the cheap hotel near the river, she was beginning to worry about the blue Volvo that was always behind her.

Mark drove past the hotel and parked a little farther along the street. Linda had got out of her van, and she looked at Mark's car as she entered the hotel. She thought she recognized the driver!

There was no one at the hotel reception desk. Linda walked up the dirty wooden stairs to room number ten, where John was waiting for her. She knocked on the door of the room.

'It's me – Linda,' she called. 'Get your things. It's time to go.'
John opened the door. His suitcase was already packed.

'Okay,' his wife said. 'Come on. Let's get moving.'

Downstairs, the reception desk was still empty. John put his room key on the desk and they left the hotel. It was completely dark outside now. As they drove away, Linda noticed that the blue Volvo was still behind them.

They crossed to the south side of the River Thames and drove on towards the port of Dover. In Dover, they would get on a ferry to France. Soon, they would be safe. But whenever Linda looked in her driving mirror, the blue car was always behind them.

————

Mark didn't care whether Linda noticed that she was being followed. He needed to keep the van in sight. But after half an hour, he saw that the van was turning off the main road. He turned off too, and soon he was following the white van along a narrow country lane.

Suddenly, the lane became even narrower and it curved sharply. On the bend, Linda stopped the van, completely blocking the way. Mark stopped a few metres behind it.

Then there was a flash in the darkness as someone fired a gun. The windscreen of Mark's car shattered and Julie screamed, falling to one side. There was blood on her coat.

In the bright beam of the Volvo's headlights, Mark saw a man running towards him, a gun in his hand. Mark put the car into reverse[4] and tried to turn round. But John Bentley was getting closer, holding the gun with both hands now and taking aim[4].

Bentley ran towards the driver's door of the car. As soon as he was close enough, Mark threw the door open, smashing it against Bentley's chest. He heard the sound of gunfire again, but he did not know where the bullet went.

John Bentley was getting closer, holding the gun with both hands now and taking aim.

Mark jumped out of the car and threw himself at Bentley. The two men fell heavily to the ground. Mark struggled to hold Bentley's arms so that he couldn't fire his gun again. Then he felt a sharp pain in his side.

Linda had come from the van and she was kicking him. A moment later, she grabbed the gun from her husband's hand and hit Mark on the back of the head with it.

As he became unconscious, he heard the woman say, 'Get into the van quickly, John! Let's get away from here!'

———

The Bentleys drove on to Dover, arriving there about an hour later. They left their van in a car-park and got onto the eleven o'clock ferry for Calais, as foot passengers[4]. John was carrying two large suitcases. Linda had a holdall. Nobody stopped them at Customs or Passport Control in Calais. A few hours later, they were racing across the French countryside on a train going south, towards Spain and freedom.

———

Mark woke several hours later in a hospital bed. At first, he didn't know where he was. There was a bandage round his aching head and he felt terribly tired.

But after a few minutes, he remembered that Julie had been shot. He called for a nurse. When the nurse came into his room, the first thing he said was, 'Where's Julie? Is she all right?'

'Don't worry, Mr Ashwood,' the nurse said. 'She'll be fine. But she's lost a lot of blood. The bullet went through her shoulder, close to her neck.'

'What happened? I can't remember anything.'

'Don't try! Sleep now,' the nurse said. 'You're both going to be all right.'

———

Some days later, Mark learnt that a motorcyclist had found him lying unconscious by his car, with Julie lying unconscious inside it. He had phoned for an ambulance and the police.

When Mark and Julie were feeling better, a police officer visited them and they both gave him statements about the attack[4]. Mark explained the whole story about Colin Fenton, and John and Linda Bentley. With this information, the police were able to connect Bentley with the robbery at Sandwell's. At first, Mark was surprised that they believed his strange story. But a policeman told him that detectives had discovered that the lock on the skylight in the roof had been broken from the *inside*, not from the outside. Also, there were no footprints on the roof, and in the shop there was a further clue. The way that the broken glass was lying in the display cabinets showed that the jewellery had been removed *before* the glass had been smashed. These clues made the police believe that it was an 'inside job' – that someone who had keys and knew the alarm code had done the robbery. The robber had reset the alarm on his way out, to confuse the police. But now, after hearing Mark's story, the police understood what had happened.

The London police reported the crime to Interpol, the international police organization. But it was too late to catch the Bentleys. By now, the police thought, they had reached the safety of Spain. They'd probably changed their names and changed the way they looked. It would take a great deal of luck to find them.

15

Officially Dead

Julie Fenton spent ten days in hospital before she was allowed to go home. When she was back at work, Mark Ashwood visited her often. Soon, he'd become her close friend. That spring, Julie stopped using Mr Booker as her accountant, and she asked Mark to look after her company's financial records instead.

One sunny evening in late May, Julie and Mark drove to a restaurant in one of the villages outside Bath. Mark had said that he wanted to take Julie to dinner and talk to her about the future of C.J.F. Software Solutions.

'I've been thinking about your problem with Jackman's,' Mark said.

'Tell me where we went wrong,' Julie said, sipping a glass of cold white wine.

'I think that, instead of trying to sell your *software* to Jackman's, and other companies like them, you should sell them licenses[1] to *use* it,' Mark said. 'You could sell licences to use the software for a period of time – perhaps a year.'

'Go on,' Julie said.

'Well, first, it's cheaper for the client,' Mark continued. 'They get the full use of the product for a year for much less than the cost of buying it. Second, if you update the product – if you make improvements to it – the licence will allow the client to have the new version free. They'll always have the latest software.'

'That's great for the client, but what about my company?' Julie asked.

'The advantage for you is client loyalty[1],' Mark replied. 'When a client's licence period ends, they won't have to buy new software, they'll just have to buy a new licence. That will be much cheaper, so the client will want to go on using *your* product, rather than buying another company's software. So the client gets regular updates, and you get loyalty. And when you do produce a completely new product, you can sell it to your existing clients at a discount[1]. It's good for both of you!'

Julie looked thoughtful. She sipped her wine again.

'I think it's a great idea,' she said at last. 'Mark, you're a genius!'

'There's another thing,' Mark went on. 'I think that all of your company's work could be done without an office. Offices are expensive. All you need is the equipment and the staff. Your staff could work at home. You'd obviously need to have regular meetings, but you could organize the work so that your staff can work independently. Your own house could be the company's official address. Your secretary would be in constant touch with you by phone. You'll save a lot of money if you don't rent an office. Your company will soon be earning well again.'

'Mark, you're wonderful,' she said. And she kissed him.

Later in the year, Mark sold his house in Stratford and he moved to Bath. He became the financial director of C.J.F. Software Solutions. By the end of the year, Julie and Mark knew that they were in love. Julie sold her house and she went to live with Mark.

Mark tried to get Julie interested in rock-climbing. At first, she didn't think she was going to like the sport. But one day, a few years after their first meeting, she was holding onto a steep rock face, with the sea far below her. Above her head, Mark was standing on a ledge, holding her rope.

'Come on up!' he shouted. 'You're doing wonderfully!'

Julie looked down at the sea and quickly closed her eyes.

But she knew that the rope was keeping her safe. As she moved slowly onwards, up the rock face, she thought, 'What am I doing here? How my life has changed! But I'm happier than I've been for years.'

———

One Sunday morning, seven years after Colin Fenton's disappearance, Mark and Julie were sitting in their garden, relaxing. Mark was looking at a book about gardening, and thinking about some new plants he wanted to grow. Julie was sitting next to him, reading a newspaper. Everything was very quiet.

Suddenly, tears came into Julie's eyes. A moment later, they were running down her cheeks. She got up quickly, leaving the paper on her chair, and walked away across the grass to the end of the garden.

Mark looked up at Julie. Her saw her drying her eyes with a handkerchief. He wondered what had made her sad. Then he noticed a photograph in the newspaper on her chair, and he knew the answer.

The photo showed two people – John and Linda Bentley. Then Mark saw the headline above it – *British Couple Arrested for Jewellery Robbery after Seven Years.*

Under the photograph, Mark read the story.

> A British couple were arrested in Spain last week in connection with crimes that took place seven years ago. They are accused of robbery and attempted murder[2]. John and Linda Bentley will fly back to Britain tomorrow to be charged[2].
>
> 'We received information from Interpol about these two people,' said Detective Inspector Williams of the London Police, who is in charge of the case. 'The Bentleys had been living in the south of Spain, using false names. They were only discovered when the woman made a claim[4] to a Spanish

She got up quickly, leaving the paper on her chair.

court. Her aunt, who also lived in Spain, had died, leaving
her property to Mrs Bentley. To claim the property, Linda
Bentley had to use her real name. That was when Interpol
found out about the couple.

'Mrs Bentley said that she was innocent of the charges.
But she did agree that the man she lived with was her husband, John Bentley, who was thought to have died seven
years ago. She said that the man whose body was cremated
as her husband's, was their friend, Mr Colin Fenton.'

Mark put the paper down. Julie walked towards him and sat
down at his side. She had stopped crying now.

'Seven years is a long time,' she said. 'A lot has happened to
me – to us. What happened seven years ago broke my life into
pieces. You helped me put the pieces together again. Colin's
death was an accident – it was nobody's fault. But when he was
cremated as John Bentley, his name was taken away from him.'

She pointed to the photograph of the Bentleys.

'It's always worried me that I didn't know how he got
involved with those people. Perhaps now I'll learn the truth.
Colin will have his own name again. At last he'll be officially
dead.'

POINTS
FOR
UNDERSTANDING
and
GLOSSARY

Points for Understanding

1

1 'For a moment, I thought I was looking in a mirror,' says Colin. Why does he say this?
2 'That guy will be useful to us,' Linda tells her husband. Why do you think she says this? How can Colin be useful to them?

2

Why do you think Colin doesn't want Julie to see the letter from Linda?

3

1 Colin is surprised by Linda's proposal. He says, 'I don't buy lottery tickets.' What does he mean by this?
2 'You planned it all, didn't you?' Colin says to Linda. What does he mean?
3 Linda has spent the night with Colin. What do you think her feelings about him are?

4

Why does Julie think that she should go to Manchester with her husband?

5

Why is Colin driving on a narrow country road when his accident happens?

6

Linda doesn't tell the police the truth about who was killed in the accident. What do you think her reasons are?

7

Colin doesn't make contact with his wife on Tuesday evening and Julie is unable to make contact with him on Wednesday. But she doesn't contact the police till Thursday. Why not?

8

1 (a) When Linda returns from identifying Colin's body, she is carrying his suitcase. She throws away some of the things in it and she keeps others. What do her choices tell you about Linda's character?
  (b) Remember your answer to Question 3 for Chapter 3. Would you now give a different answer? Why?
2 'You've taken my life away from me,' John Bentley says to Linda. What does he mean by this?

9

'Julie was shocked, but she was beginning to understand.' What was she beginning to understand?

10

1 Mark visits Linda Bentley, but he feels foolish and wishes he hadn't come. Why is this?
2 Mark sees an advertisement in a newspaper. 'There's certainly a puzzle here,' Mark thinks. 'But perhaps I'm beginning to solve it.' Why does he think this?

11

Mark is telling Julie about Linda Bentley. After Julie says, 'And her husband was alive and well, I suppose?', Mark knows what she is thinking and what she is going to say next. Explain what Julie is thinking.

12

John Bentley wants the police to think that the robbers have broken into Sandwell's from the outside. Explain the things he does to make them think this.

13

By the end of this chapter, Julie believes Mark's ideas about the car accident. What things have made her change her mind?

14

If Frankie Simpson has sold the jewellery for half a million pounds, and if he keeps the agreed amount for himself, how many bundles of banknotes does he give Linda?

15

'Colin will have his own name again,' Julie says at the end of the book. What does she mean?

Glossary

Terms to do with business

arranged a loan (page 12)

Colin is going to borrow some money from a bank so that he can buy the things that he needs for the company and so he can pay the staff. The bank will *charge interest on the loan*. This extra money will have to be paid after the loan is repaid.

client loyalty (page 93)

clients pay someone, or a company, to work for them. When clients ask the same company to work for them over many years, these clients are being *loyal* to that company. C.J.F. Software Solutions will earn money regularly if they keep the same clients for many years.

computer software (page 5)

software is the set of instructions given to a computer that makes it complete its work. Colin is training business people to use the instructions on their computers correctly. He is teaching a *course in computer software*.

confirmed – *waiting for a valuable contract to be confirmed* (page 56)

Colin is waiting for one of the companies that he is working for to contact him. Colin's company has developed some *software* (see above) for this company. When the company agrees to Colin's price for the work, they will *confirm the contract* and the agreement will be legal. There has been a lot of work for Colin to do for this contract and he will earn a lot of money from it.

deal (page 62)

an agreement between two people, or two companies, that they will do business together.

discount – *sell at a discount* (page 94)

sell products for less than their usual price.

export regulations (page 43)

the rules that businesses have to follow when they send goods overseas to sell them. The *Department of Trade and Industry* is the section of the British Government which prepares these rules. The department publishes these rules in books. The officers of the D.T.I. make sure that companies follow these rules.

floppy disks (page 14)

    copies of documents or files from a computer can be stored on these thin, flat pieces of metal and plastic.

go out of business (page 12)

    to be unsuccessful in business and have to close your company.

insurance brokers (page 12)

    a company that makes arrangements for *insurance*. People or businesses can be *insured* so that if there is damage to property or someone is injured in an accident, they will be paid some money. To get insurance, a sum of money has to be paid every year to an *insurance company*. *Insurance brokers* find the best prices for this kind of arrangement. Then they make sure that the insurance company pays the person or business that has had trouble.

licences (page 93)

    special agreements which allow people to use a company's product or idea. The *licence* is the document which describes this agreement. It says how long the agreement will last – the *licence period* (page 93). All computer software (see above) is *licensed* to the people who want to use it. If the computer company develops a newer *version* (page 93) of the software, then the users need another agreement.

main stock (page 76)

    goods that are to be sold. The *main stock* in Sandwell's is the expensive jewellery which is put in the strong-room every night.

profits (page 43)

    the money that a company earns after all the expenses have been paid.

programmers (page 14)

    people who work with computers. *Programmers* prepare the instructions that make computers complete different types of work.

raise that much cash (page 62)

    Frankie is saying that it will be difficult for him to sell a million pounds' worth of stolen jewellery quickly. He will have to speak to many people before he has sold all the jewellery and has got the money.

SECTION 2
Terms to do with crime and criminals

a chance to live an honest life (page 17)
> the manager at Sandwell's thought that John was not going to steal again. He gave him a job so that he would be able to earn money honestly and he would no longer be a criminal.

alibi (page 23)
> if you are accused of a crime and you can prove to the police that you were not where the crime took place, this is *an alibi*. If someone can also tell the police that your information is correct – prove that your story is true – they can *provide you with* or *give you an alibi* (page 26).

attempted murder (page 95)
> when someone tries to kill another person but does not succeed, this is the crime of *attempted murder*.

break-in (page 24)
> when somebody gets into a house, shop or office building by breaking a door or a window and steals something.

charged (page 95)
> when criminals are arrested by the police, they are *charged*. They are told what their crime is and they are later taken to court.

criminal record (page 24)
> the details – the *record* – of all of a criminal's crimes are kept by the police.

fence (page 27)
> a criminal *fences* – buys or sells stolen things – to or from another person. The criminal who buys or sells these things is called a *fence* (page 79).

plastic explosive (page 78)
> a soft material that is pushed onto wood, metal or stone to break them apart with an explosion. A *detonator* (page 78) has to be put into the material to make it explode. The detonator explodes using electricity. A *timer* (page 78) is used so that the explosion happens at a particular time. John has to *set the timer of the detonator* (page 78) carefully so that the plastic explosive breaks open the lock of the door at the right time.

security systems (page 24)
> equipment that is put into shops, houses or offices to stop thieves stealing things from them. The *alarm* (page 24) usually has *bells* (page 75) which ring if someone breaks a window or an outside door. Shops or banks often have alarm bells which will ring at the

nearest police station if someone tries to get into the buildings. Security systems work using electricity. Secret numbers – a *code* (page 75) – are put into the device by using a *keypad* (page 75). A keypad looks like the front of a calculator. When the code is entered on the keypad and the system is switched on, the security alarm is working. The code number has to be re-entered on the keypad to turn the security system off.

In Sandwell's shop there is an *electronic combination lock* (page 76) on the door of the strong-room. The heavy, powerful lock opens and shuts using electricity. There is no metal key for the lock. The door is locked and unlocked when secret numbers are entered on a keypad. If the door is opened, the lock has to be *reset* (page 78) to make it safe.

small-time thieving (page 9)

Linda is saying that John will no longer be stealing small amounts of money or less valuable things as he did in the past.

SECTION 3
Colloquial language

a hell of a lot of jewellery (page 62)

an extremely large amount of jewellery.

be in touch (page 24)

this means, I will speak to you on the phone. See also *get in touch* (page 37). This means, If you phone me, we will be able to have a discussion. These phrases mean the same as *to be/get in contact* with someone.

get down to business (page 62)

this means, Shall we start talking about our business?

get rid of (page 50)

this means, I'm going to drive Colin's car away from the house and leave it somewhere where it will only be found after a long time.

go missing (page 46)

disappear.

I'd better be going (page 14)

this means, I must leave now or I will be late.

mates (page 19)

friends.

sort out (page 11)

find answers to the problems on the computer software.

What's your game? (page 9)

　　this means, What trick are you trying to play on me? John thinks
　　that Linda is being too friendly towards Colin.

Where the hell is he? (page 44)

　　Julie is nervous and worried because she hasn't been able to speak
　　to Colin. This strong way of speaking shows her feelings.

SECTION 4
General

abandoned (page 47)

　　left someone or something without telling anyone where you were
　　going.

accent (page 6)

　　the way you speak English. John Bentley comes from south-east
　　London. He speaks with a *soft London accent.*

appreciate (page 66)

　　be very grateful for the things someone has done.

attack (page 92)

　　the time when the Bentleys tried to injure and kill Mark and
　　Julie.

attend an inquest (page 37)

　　when someone dies suddenly, an official has to find out how and
　　why they died. This is called an *inquest.* People who knew the dead
　　person, or were present when they died, go to a special meeting.
　　They *attend an inquest* and an official asks them questions.

boot (page 29)

　　the place behind the rear seats of a car where you can carry things.

breakdown truck (page 36)

　　a powerful truck which pulls vehicles that have been in an acci-
　　dent, or which cannot be driven, to a garage to be repaired.

car jack (page 74)

　　a tool used to lift a car from the ground when you want to change
　　the tyre on one of its wheels. A *car jack* has a long handle which
　　you push up and down to lift the car.

claim (page 95)

　　Linda Bentley has gone to a court of law in Spain and said that her
　　aunt has died. She has told the court her real name and said that
　　she should have her aunt's money. She has made a *claim.*

common – *had something in common* (page 16)

neither John nor Linda's parents were alive when they first met each other. The thing that they *had in common* was that they were both orphans. This phrase can also be used for people who have the same interests and like the same kind of things.

connect – *connect that with* (page 41)

Linda is saying that nobody will think about a funeral for John Bentley and believe that it has anything to do with a man called Colin Fenton, who has disappeared.

contacts in the jewellery trade (page 63)

Frankie knows many people who buy and sell jewellery. These *contacts* help criminals to buy and to sell stolen jewellery or they give criminals information about jewellery in shops.

cutting equipment (page 33)

machines which can cut through strong metal.

display cabinets (page 78)

large cupboards with glass tops which are used to show the goods that are for sale in a shop.

disturb – *sorry to disturb you* (page 39)

the police officers are saying that they are sorry to come to Linda's house late at night.

emergency services (page 33)

organizations which help people who are in trouble or in danger. The three main emergency services are Fire, Ambulance and Police. In Britain, you can ask for help from the emergency services by phoning the number 999. A *fire crew* (page 33) travel in a *fire engine* (page 35). Fire crews help people who cannot escape from vehicles, buildings, rivers etc. They put out fires. They also use *cutting equipment* (see above). An *ambulance* (page 33) is called for when someone is ill and has to go to hospital. *Paramedics* (page 35) travel in ambulances. They help injured people. A *stretcher* (page 36) is used to carry an injured person to and from an ambulance. The *police* (page 31) stop people breaking laws, they arrest criminals and help people who are in trouble.

exit (page 29)

the place where you can leave a motorway and drive onto smaller roads.

flirting (page 9)

behaving towards someone in a way that shows you like them very much.

foot passengers (page 91)

passengers who walk onto a ferry boat. They are taking a journey across the sea without a car, a bus, a coach or a truck.

frost (page 23)

hard, white ice which covers everything – roads, vehicles, buildings, grass, trees and plants – when the weather is very cold.

funeral (page 41)

the ceremony that takes place after someone dies. People who die are either *cremated* (page 51) or *buried* (page 84) in the ground. When a dead person is cremated, the body is burnt and the only thing that is left is soft dust – *ashes* (page 51). The *cremation* takes place in a building called a *crematorium* (page 51). The relatives of the dead person sometimes have the ashes *scattered* (page 51). This means that the ashes are put on the ground or sometimes, onto water. Relatives often like to scatter the ashes in a place that the dead person enjoyed visiting.

fussy (page 28)

want work to be completed in a particular way. Someone who is *fussy* likes everything to be tidy and correct.

getting to know each other – *spent time getting to know each other* (page 20)

talked together and found out about each others' lives and what they like and dislike.

identify the body (page 37)

go to a hospital or a police station to look at the body of a dead person and say who they are and where they lived. This is called *identification* (page 37). It is usually relatives who are asked to identify a body. Someone's *identity* (page 48) is the information about their name, age, address, their family and what sort of person they are. This information is kept in official records, together with details about their health and the money they have paid to the government for taxes.

involved – *to be involved with* (page 82)

know and work with someone.

junction (page 30)

the place where you can get onto or leave a motorway.

lay-by (page 29)

a place where vehicles can stop beside a road.

lined with (page 9)

there are shops along both sides of the road.

109

mass – *a mass of torn metal* (page 33)

the car has been so badly damaged that it just looks like a huge piece of metal.

officially dead (page 53)

when someone is *officially dead* the date of their death is put on that person's tax records, medical records and personal documents.

out of control (page 32)

the driver of the car cannot keep the car travelling safely on the road. The car is *out of control*.

Passport Authority (page 86)

the government department that prepares passports for British people who want to travel from Britain. All the information given on a passport must be correct or this official document is not legal. Relatives inform the Passport Authority when someone in their family dies, so that the passport is cancelled.

picked one at random (page 57)

Julie takes a CD quickly, without looking carefully at it.

proposal (page 20)

suggest to someone that you do something together. Colin had been expecting a *proposal* from Linda that they should make love together.

put the car into reverse (page 89)

Mark moves the gear controls of the car and drives it backwards.

puzzled – *to look puzzled* (page 56)

the expression on your face when you do not understand something.

reaction (page 70)

the way you behave when you hear good or bad news. Your reaction could be happiness, sadness, fear, shock or anger.

receipts (page 82)

pieces of paper that you are given when you buy goods or services. The *receipt* shows how much you paid for the goods or the services, and when you bought them.

rented (page 17)

a house that does not belong to the person who lives there. The agreement between the owner and the person who *rents* the house is called a *lease*. When the person no longer wants to live in that house, the *lease is cancelled* (page 53).

risk – *know what risk I'll be taking* (page 23)

Colin wants to know how serious the crime is that John and Linda are planning. He wants to know if he might go to prison, if they are caught by the police.

roadworks (page 32)

the place on a road or a motorway where workmen are using machines to repair it.

second year running (page 12)

for two years, Colin's company has not earnt enough money.

self-control (page 60)

a person with *self-control* waits and thinks carefully before they do anything.

service area (page 29)

the buildings at the side of a motorway where you can stop and eat a meal in a restaurant or buy fuel for your car.

sideboard (page 19)

a long cupboard in a dining-room where glasses, plates, knives, forks and spoons are usually kept.

sign a statement (page 37)

when there is an accident or a crime, police officers ask people who have any information to write down a *statement*. This gives details of everything that the person knows about the crime or the accident. The person then *signs the statement* to show that everything they have written is true.

steel shutter (page 75)

a strong metal cover that is pulled down over the doors and windows of a shop or a building in which valuable things are kept.

suburbs (page 5)

the area outside the centre of a city.

sympathize (page 50)

listen to someone's troubles and tell them that you are sorry that these things have happened.

taking aim (page 89)

John is carefully pointing a gun at Mark because he is going to shoot him.

wallet (page 15)

a leather container for holding banknotes.

witnessed – *to be witness to* (page 32)

the person who sees an accident happen has *witnessed* an accident. The police may ask the *witness* to describe what happened – give a statement. Later, the person may have to go to a court of law and say what they saw.

Yellow Pages (page 15)

a British reference book which gives addresses and phone numbers for businesses and services.

Exercises

Grammar Focus 1: *who* and *which*

Read the story outline. Then join the sentences below using *who* or *which*.

Colin Fenton and his wife Julie were the owners of a small computer firm called C.J.F. Software Solutions. Julie wrote business software at their offices in Bath, in the west of England. Colin travelled around the country marketing the software and teaching the programs to administrative staff.

During a visit to Brentwood, a town close to London, Colin went into a pub where he met John and Linda Bentley. Linda was very attractive. Linda noticed immediately that Colin looked exactly like her husband. The two men's faces were similar: they even had similar hairstyles. Linda worked in a jewellery store, and when she saw Colin, she had an idea for a robbery.

1 C.J.F. Software Solutions was a small company. C.J.F. was based in Bath.
   C.J.F. Software Solutions was a small company which was based in Bath.

2 Colin Fenton owned the firm with his wife Julie. She was a software developer.
   Colin Fenton owned the firm with his wife Julie, who was a software developer.

3 One day Colin went to Brentwood. Brentwood is a small town close to London.

   ....

   ....

4 Colin went into a pub. The pub was showing a football match.

   ....

   ....

112

5   Colin met John Bentley. John looked exactly like him.

....

....

6   Colin also met John's wife Linda. She was very attractive.

....

....

7   Linda worked in a jewellery store. It specialised in diamonds.

....

....

8   Linda had an idea for a robbery. It involved the two men.

....

....

Grammar Focus 2: *the same as* and *similar to*

Look at the information below. Write sentences comparing John and Colin, using *the same as* or *similar to*.

1   John was 182 cms tall. Colin was 182 cms tall.
    John was the same height as Colin.

2   John had fair hair. Colin had blond hair.
    John's hair was

3   John wore light blue jeans. Colin wore faded blue jeans.
    John's jeans were

4   John's middle name was Thomas. Colin's middle name was Thomas.
    John's middle name was

5   John was 28 years old. Colin was 28 years old.
    John was

6   John's star sign was Capricorn. Colin's star sign was Capricorn.
    John's star sign was

A Visit to the Accountant's

Complete the gaps. Use each word or phrase in the box once.

> go out of   face   temporary   orders   cash   do
> down   documents   facts   earned   raised   spent   pleased
> folder   pain   briefly   lose   running   moment
> situation   floor   glasses   survive

Mr Booker wore very thick ¹......*glasses*...... and he held the papers very close to his pale ²........................... . He looked like a man in ³........................... .

Colin sat ⁴........................... and pushed a folder of financial ⁵........................... across the desk. Booker slowly ⁶........................... his head, opened the ⁷........................... and glanced ⁸........................... through the documents.

'You're going to ⁹........................... money for the second year ¹⁰..........................., Mr Fenton,' he said. 'You've got to ¹¹........................... something about this quickly or you'll ¹²........................... business.'

'I know the ¹³........................... isn't good at the ¹⁴........................... ,' Colin replied. 'We're short of ¹⁵........................... . But the situation's only ¹⁶........................... .

'Well,' Booker said, 'the ¹⁷........................... are clear enough. This year, you've ¹⁸........................... around £40,000 so far. But last year, you ¹⁹........................... more than £150,000. And you'll spend more or less the same this year. Your business won't ²⁰........................... unless there are some large ²¹........................... coming in soon.'

Colin was silent. He looked down at the ²²........................... .

Booker leant forward. 'And you haven't got any large orders coming in, have you?' he said. He seemed almost ²³........................... .

114

Words and Structures

Tick the best answer.

1 What is an *accountant* concerned with?
a ☐ Finding new staff for a business.
b ☐ Writing business software.
c ☐ Selling a company's products.
d ☑ The income and expenditure of a company.

2 What is an adjective for *money matters*?
a ☐ Commercial.
b ☐ Financial.
c ☐ Secretarial.
d ☐ Clerical.

3 Why did Mr Booker *look like a man in pain*?
a ☐ Because he had been sitting down for too long and had cramp.
b ☐ Because his job was very boring.
c ☐ Because he was short-sighted and held papers too near his face.
d ☐ Because he did not get enough exercise and his clothes were too tight.

4 What is the opposite of *lose money* in terms of business profits?
a ☐ make money
b ☐ win money
c ☐ find money
d ☐ keep money

5 Colin says, 'I know the situation isn't good at the moment.' What is the best synonym for *situation* here?
a ☐ job
b ☐ position
c ☐ circumstance
d ☐ balance

6 Another way of saying *You will go out of business* is
a ☐ Your business will have to move.
b ☐ You will find it very difficult to get new clients.
c ☐ Your business will become bankrupt.
d ☐ You will no longer be recognised by bigger companies.

7 *The situation is only temporary.* What is another way of saying this?
a ☐ These things aren't important.
b ☐ This will not last long.
c ☐ This isn't taking much time.
d ☐ This is a long-term position.

Words From the Story

Unjumble the letters to find words from the story. Then complete the sentences below.

> sorpopal   dentiepurex   emportray   endabodan
> stewins   piercest   crysuite   clanfinai
> crimfon   recscan   findyeti   cantcost

1 One difference between John and Colin was that they spoke with different ....*accents*........ .

2 Colin gave all his business .... to Mr Booker to show how much he had spent.

3 Linda knew that Frankie Simpson had many criminal .... who could sell stolen jewellery.

4 The police asked Linda to .... her dead husband's body.

5 Mark Ashwood was the only person to .... Colin's car crash. He made a statement to the police.

116

6 Linda made a .... to Colin: she offered him £10,000 to be her husband's alibi at the time of the jewel robbery.

7 Linda worked at Sandwell's, so she knew all about the .... system which guarded the strong-room.

8 Linda and John .... their car at Dover and got on a ferry to France. They never came back.

9 Before she could inherit her aunt's property, Linda had to .... her real identity.

10 Colin needed to borrow some money for a short time. He asked the bank for a .... loan.

11 Profit is the balance of income over ....

12 Mr Booker said that Colin's .... situation was very serious.

Multiple Choice

Tick the best answer.

1 Why didn't Colin discuss the meeting he had had with Booker when he saw Julie?
a ☐ Because he had a lot of work to do that afternoon.
b ☐ Because they always discussed financial matters at home.
c ☑ Because Julie wasn't aware that the company was in financial difficulty.

2 Why was the jewellery robbery planned for January?
a ☐ Because Colin had a business trip arranged then.
b ☐ Because robberies are easier to carry out in cold weather.
c ☐ Because Frankie Simpson needed the jewellery as soon as possible after Christmas.

3 Why couldn't Julie contact Colin at his hotel in Manchester when he disappeared?

a ☐ Because he had never checked in.

b ☐ Because he had made the reservation himself and his secretary hadn't asked for the details.

c ☐ Because he had cancelled the reservation and gone to stay with the Bentleys instead.

4 What did Mr Booker think had happened to Colin?

a ☐ He thought he had been murdered.

b ☐ He thought he had run away because of his financial problems.

c ☐ He thought he had moved in with another woman.

5 Why did Julie think Mr Booker might be wrong?

a ☐ Because Colin had disappeared before the contract with Jackman's fell through.

b ☐ Because she knew that Colin had plenty of money in savings.

c ☐ Because Colin never worried about money.

6 How had Mark Ashwood found out Linda Bentley's address?

a ☐ Colin had given it to him before he died.

b ☐ The police had agreed to give it to him after they had identified the dead man's body.

c ☐ The police had given it to him on the day of the accident.

7 Why was Mark confused when he visited the Bentleys?

a ☐ Because the dying man had described his wife, and Mrs Bentley didn't look like his description.

b ☐ Because he thought the dying man had been very fond of his wife, and Mrs Bentley said they had not had a happy marriage.

c ☐ Because the dying man had given him a message for his wife Julie, and Mrs Bentley was called Linda.

8 Why didn't Julie believe Mark Ashwood when he told her that Colin had been killed in a car crash?

a ☐ Because Colin's BMW had just been found at Heathrow Airport.

b ☐ Because she knew he couldn't have been in Oxfordshire on the day of the accident.

c ☐ Because he said that the accident happened at ten o'clock, and her husband was still at home at that time.

9   Why did Julie begin to think that Mark might have been right
    about the car crash?
a   ☐ Because she had a phone call from Linda Bentley.
b   ☐ Because she heard about the robbery at the jewellery store and
       realised what had happened.
c   ☐ Because she found Colin's passport, so she knew he hadn't left
       the country.

10 Why were the police not surprised when Mark told them the story
    about Colin Fenton and the Bentleys?
a   ☐ Because Interpol had caught the Bentleys on their way to Spain.
b   ☐ Because they believed that the Sandwell's robbery was an 'inside
       job', and John Bentley was an obvious suspect.
c   ☐ Because several people had seen John Bentley on the ferry to
       France.

11 How were John and Linda Bentley finally caught?
a   ☐ Linda Bentley revealed her real name in order to claim an
       inheritance.
b   ☐ Someone from Interpol spotted them in Spain.
c   ☐ They were caught trying to carry out another robbery in Spain.

Macmillan Education
Between Towns Road, Oxford OX4 3PP
A divison of Macmillan Publishers Limited
Companies and representatives throughout the world

ISBN 978–0–230–03053–4
ISBN 978–1–4050–7684–5 (with CD edition)

Illustrated by Fiona MacVicar
Original cover template design by Jackie Hill
Cover illustration by Neil Leslie

Printed in Thailand

with CD edition
2015 2014 2013
19 18 17 16

without CD edition
2015 2014 2013
10 9 8 7 6